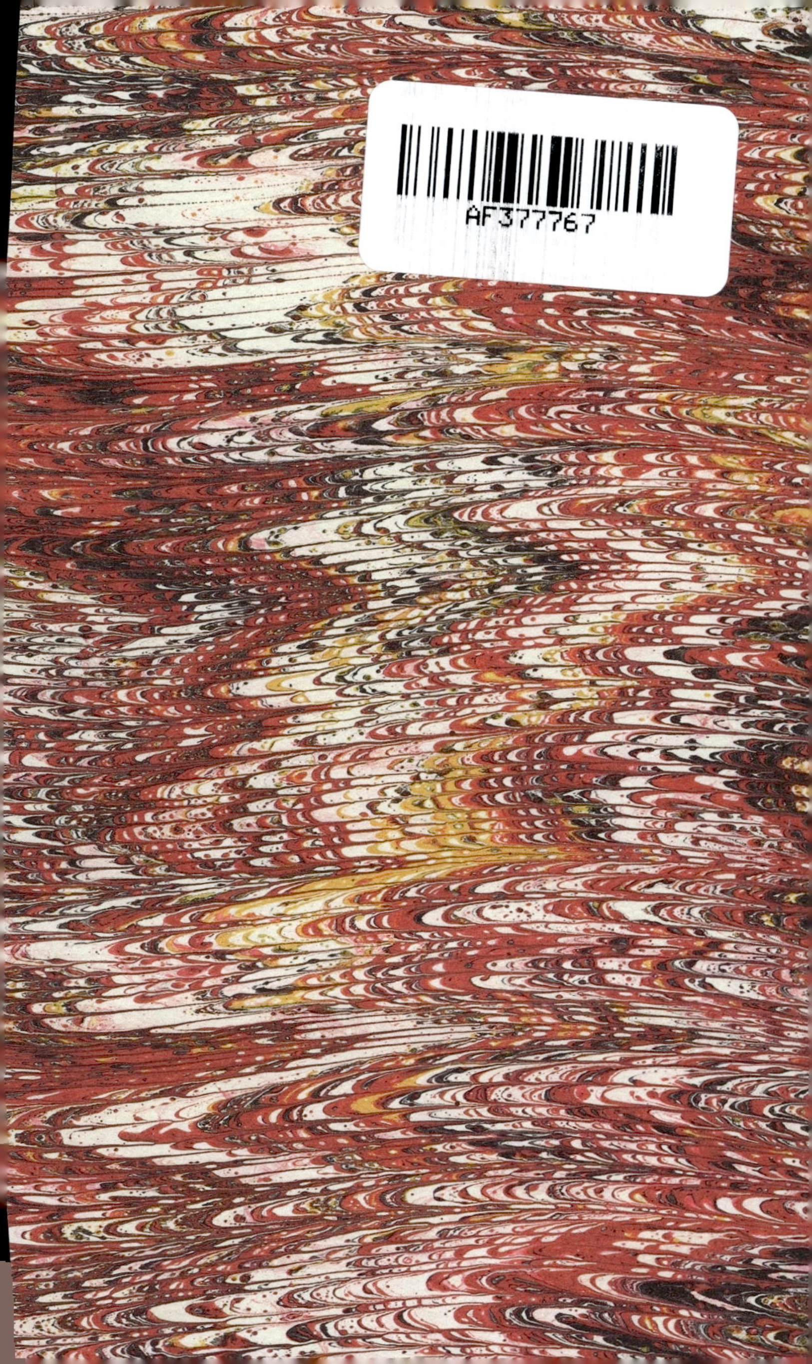

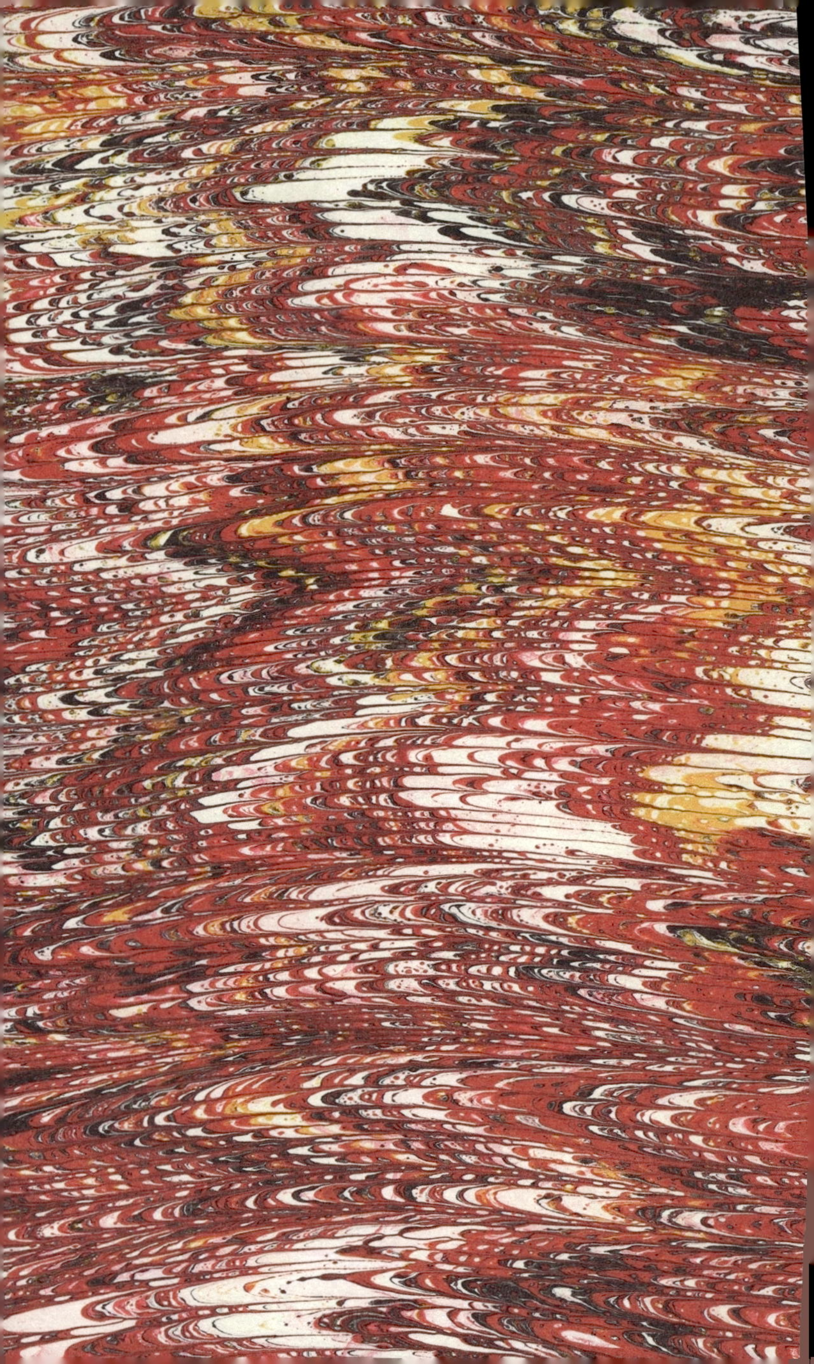

ANIMAL SPIRITS

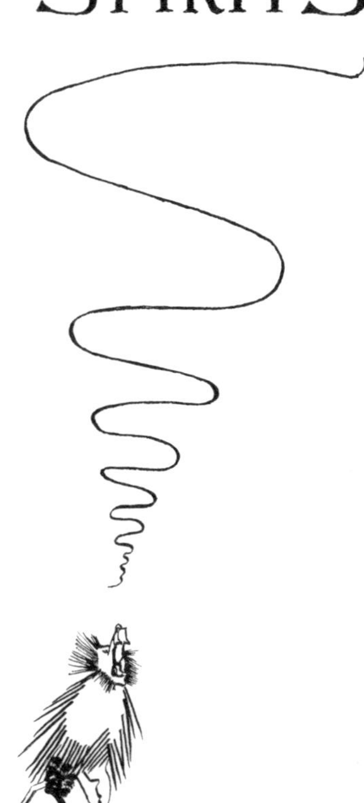

Fables in the Parlance of our times

Composed,
Queried,
Clarified,
Distilled,
&
Told Anew

by

Michael Stevenson

&

Jan Verwoert

Done Into Pictures

by

Margaret & Michael Stevenson

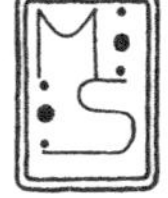

Made Into a
Book

by

CHRISTOPH KELLER

Printed by
DZA Druckerei zu Altenburg GmbH

This book is part of the
Christoph Keller Editions series
published by

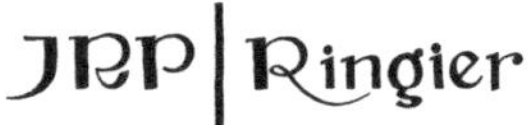

Zurich

ISBN 978-3-03764-137-8

in collaboration with

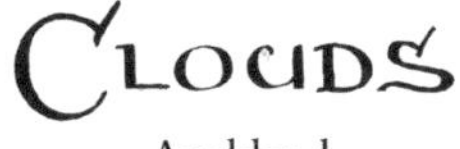

Auckland

ISBN 978-0-9582981-6-2

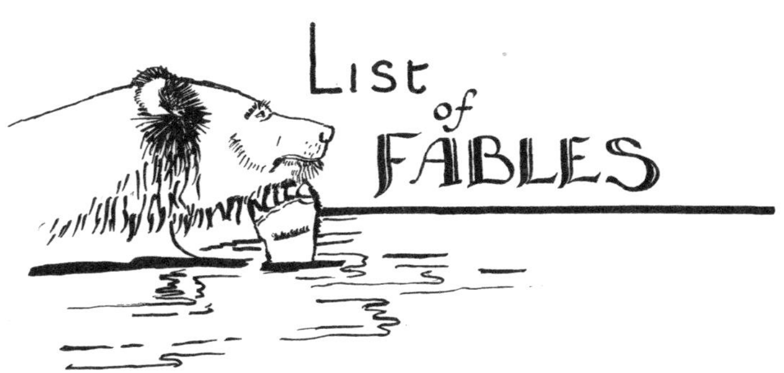

List of Fables

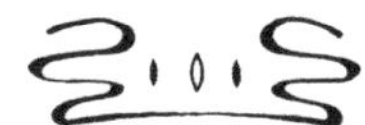

ANIMAL SPIRITS

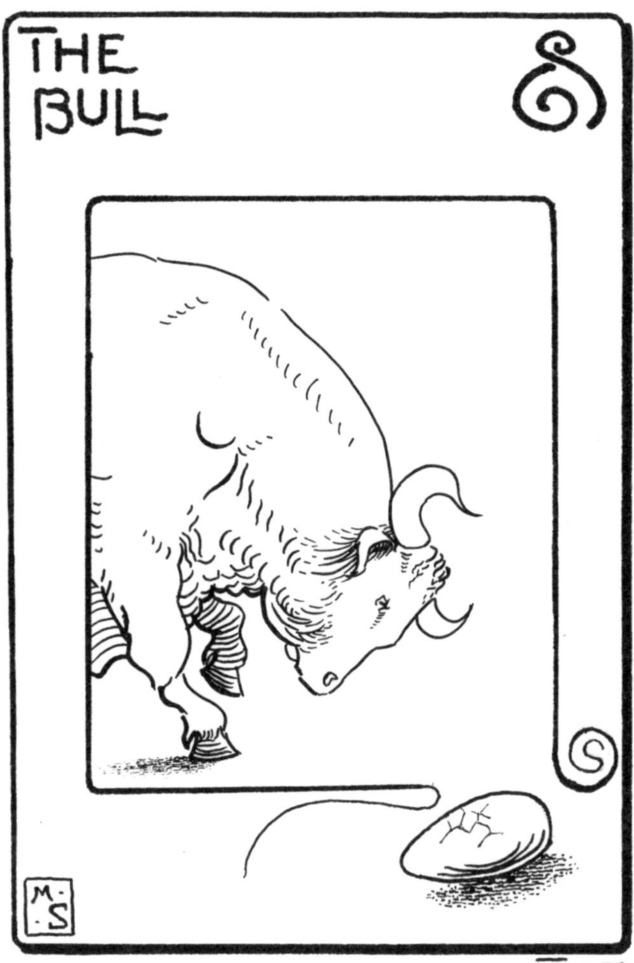

THE
BULL

M
S

THE
BEGINNING
OF THE
WORLD

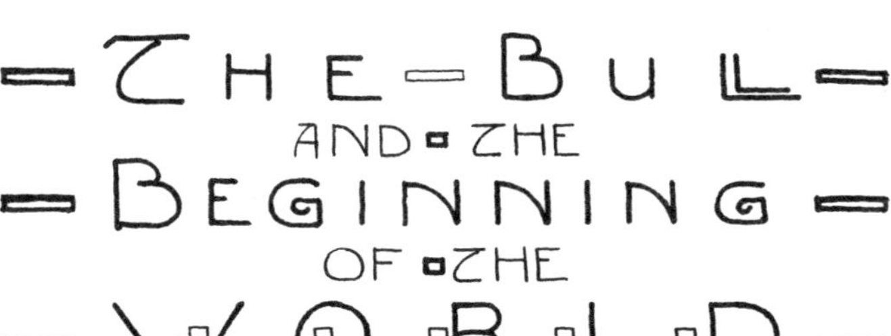

THE BULL AND THE BEGINNING OF THE WORLD

LEAVING THE PASTURES one evening the Bull came upon the Beginning of the World resting peacefully in the fading light of the day.

"Who are you to sit in my way!" roared the Bull as he stamped the ground with his hoofs. "Move or I will end your miserable life with one powerful thrust of my horns!"

"Do as you please," the Beginning of the World replied calmly, "but behold! When you do to me what you are threatening, the end of this day will be the end of your days too, for never again will there be a new beginning."

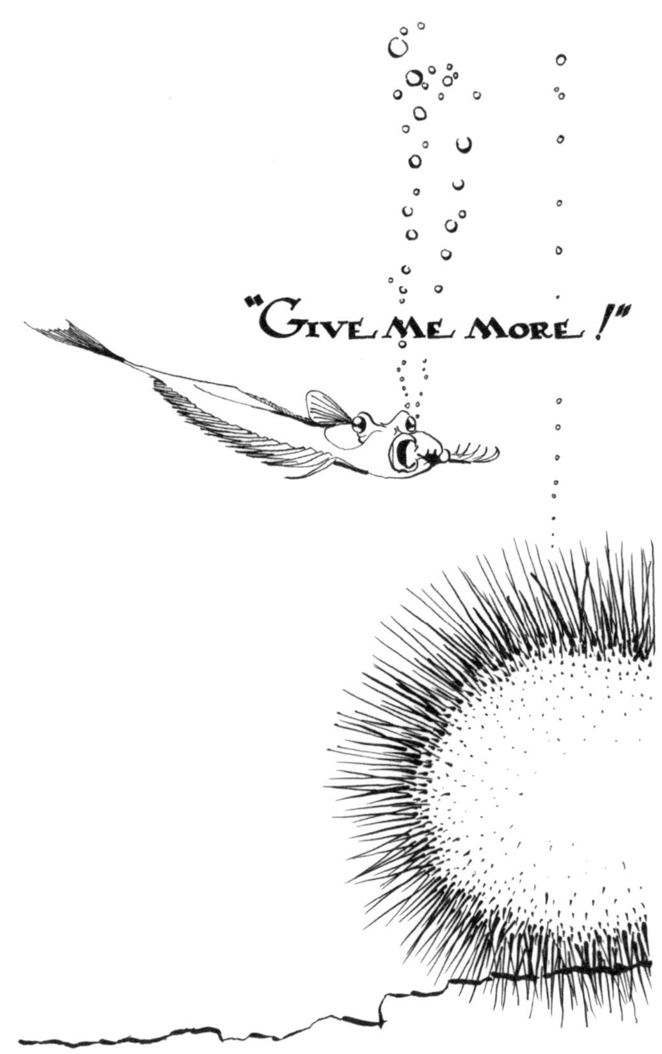
"Give Me More!"

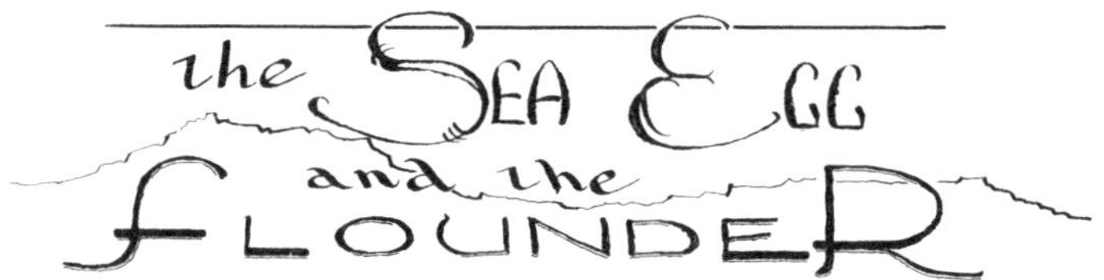

"GIVE ME MORE! I want more!" the Flounder cried, splayed out on the bottom of the ocean.

A bulbous Sea Egg, nestling on a rock nearby, felt touched by the call and promptly answered: "Since I have a lot, it would be a pleasure to give you some."

"Oh no! Not you!" the Flounder exclaimed, shuddering with repulsion. "When the round-bodied likes of you say you want to give 'some,' it usually means all you have, and that is too much for any fish to handle. So thank you, but no!"

Deeply upset by this unexpected response the Sea Egg could only stammer, "But you, you cried for more!"

"I did," the Flounder explained. "Yet what I meant was just a little more, not more than I want, and just enough of what I need. All in balanced measure!"

Poseidon witnessed the scene and shook his head in dismay.

"Oh, holy crayfish," he muttered, "what nonsense! If some are vain enough to think they had something to share, and others mortally fear to change their diet, then perhaps we should all do just as we please. Those full of themselves can burst, and the cautious can starve, as they will, each according to their own proper standards."

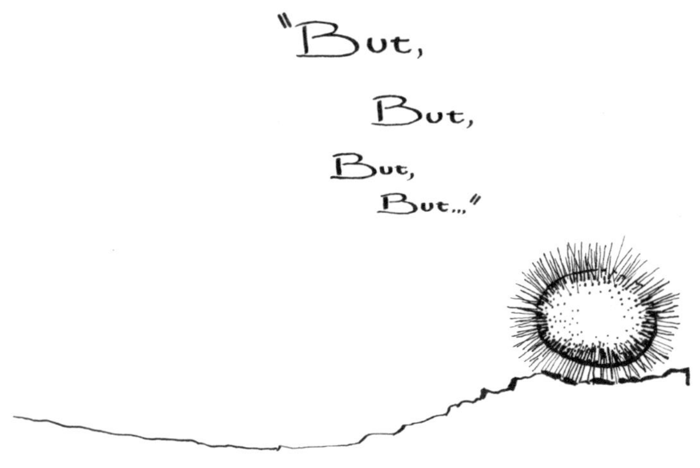

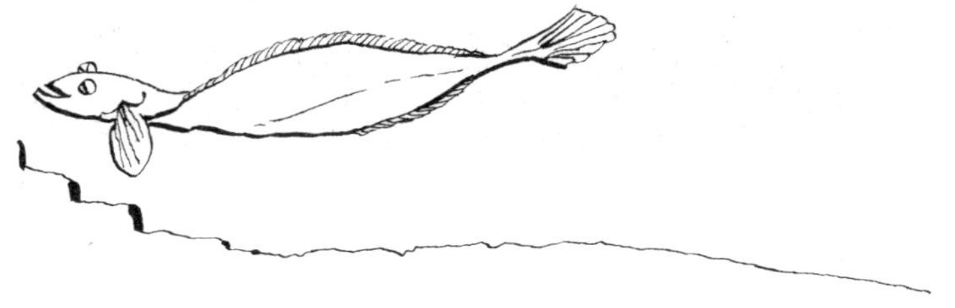

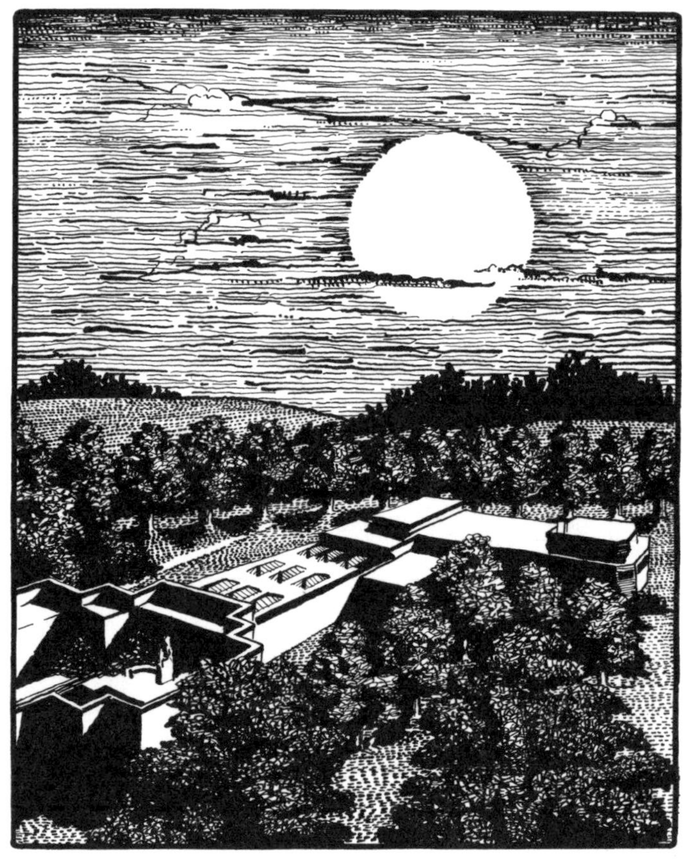

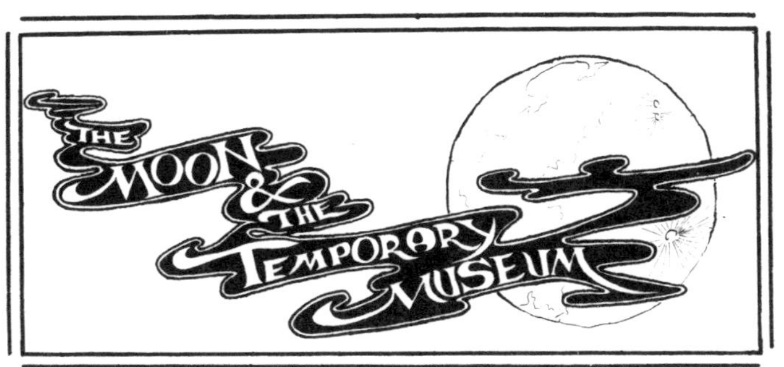

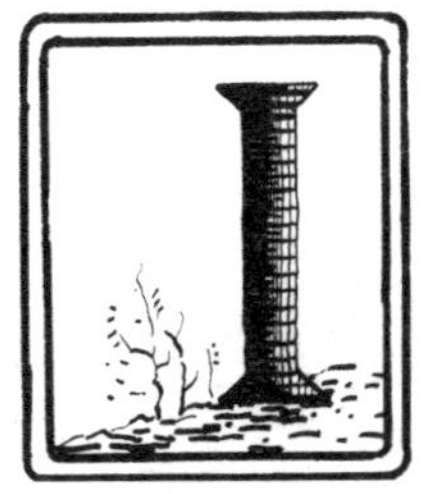

IN THE EARLY HOURS of the morning the Moon gazed down at the Temporary Museum and was surprised to see that she was already awake.

"Why don't you go back to sleep? It's hours before your opening time," said the Moon soothingly in her soft, calm voice.

"I know, I know," the Temporary Museum replied nervously. "It's easy for you to say that. For you every night is like any other. You go up and down and up again. But for me things are different. I am only temporary. So I can never be sure what the future brings. This is why I like to be up early, to be prepared for what may happen on the new day."

The Moon thought about this for a day and half of a night. When she noticed that the Museum began to stir in the early hours of the next night, she spoke again:

"Listen, I have thought about what you told me last night and I see why you are worried. But what I cannot understand is how waking up early could prepare you for what the future brings?"

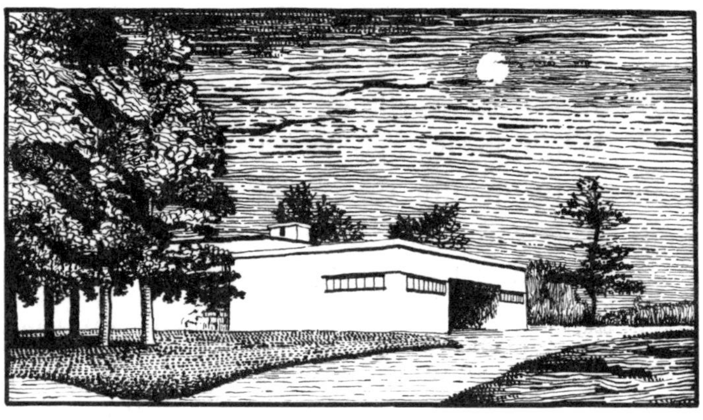

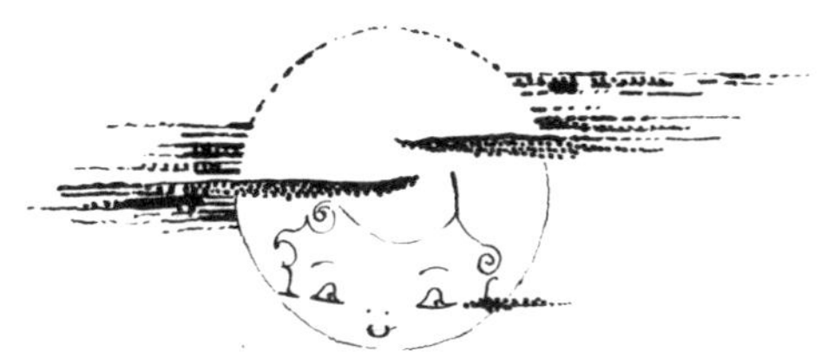

As the Temporary Museum didn't know how to reply, another day, and half of the next night passed without a word being passed between the Moon and the Museum.

Finally the Museum made up her mind and said, "All my life I have had to present myself in public knowing that I am a mere shadow of the building that was originally planned. My masters always dreamed of a much grander, more elegant design. I came to be only when the ideal was no longer possible. You see it was only out of desperation that I was built, and I am still only temporary. My walls are made well enough but it burdens me to live with this knowledge. Since I cannot rest anyhow, instead of worrying about all of the reasons for this state of affairs, I use the early hours to prepare a good mood for the visitors."

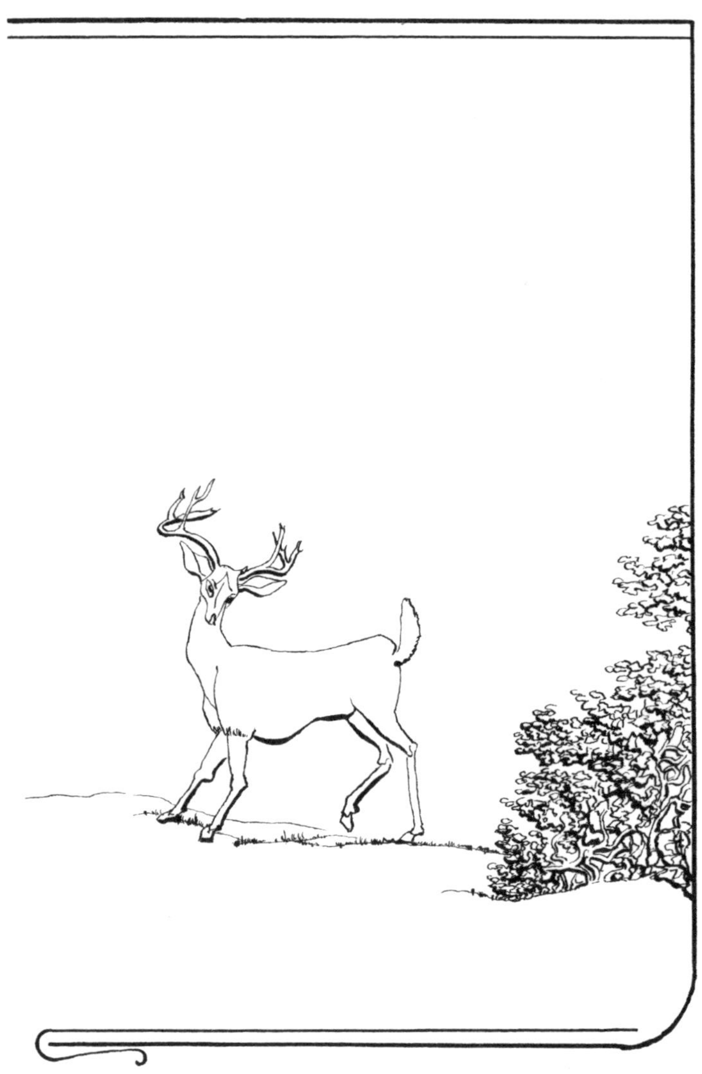

THE STAG AND THE HEDGE

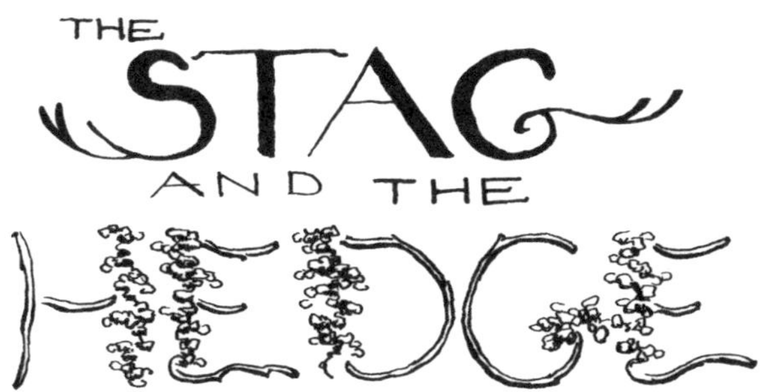

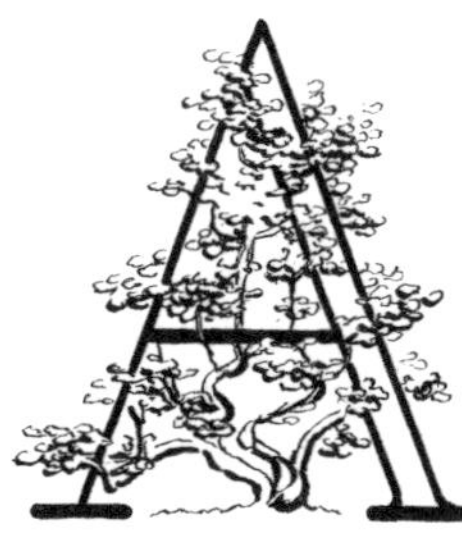

A STAG, OFF TO GRAZE in the meadows, would by habit call in at the boundary Hedge and linger a while amongst its enveloping foliage. Each day it silently made this precautionary stop and then continued on, without incident. After some months, the perturbed Hedge finally spoke when again the Stag returned to nestle.

"What is it you expect of me?" it enquired.

"Cover!" replied the Stag. "This is all I ask."

"Since I see everything from my position, I have provided you something beyond that of simple cover," responded the Hedge in a clipped tone.

"For if you had dashed off at an untimely moment, I would have reeled you back. All this constant invigilation however has turned me into a densely entwined mass. My boughs are contorted from the turning back and forth on your behalf."

"On my behalf?" returned the perplexed Stag. "Would you not have done the same for the Boar, the Hare or the Pheasant?"

Silence fell before the Hedge resumed with grief in its voice, "I did what I did for you alone... but what good is it now if you don't see this?"

"None at all, I'm afraid," quipped the Stag wandering off.

"See you again tomorrow."

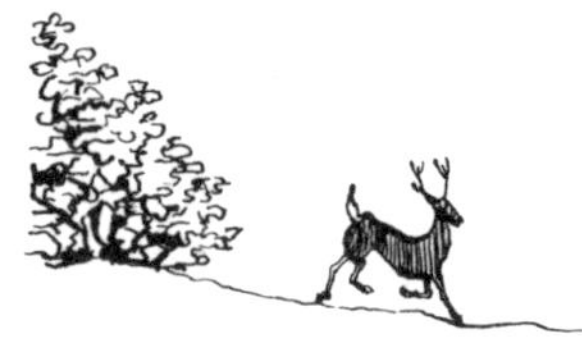

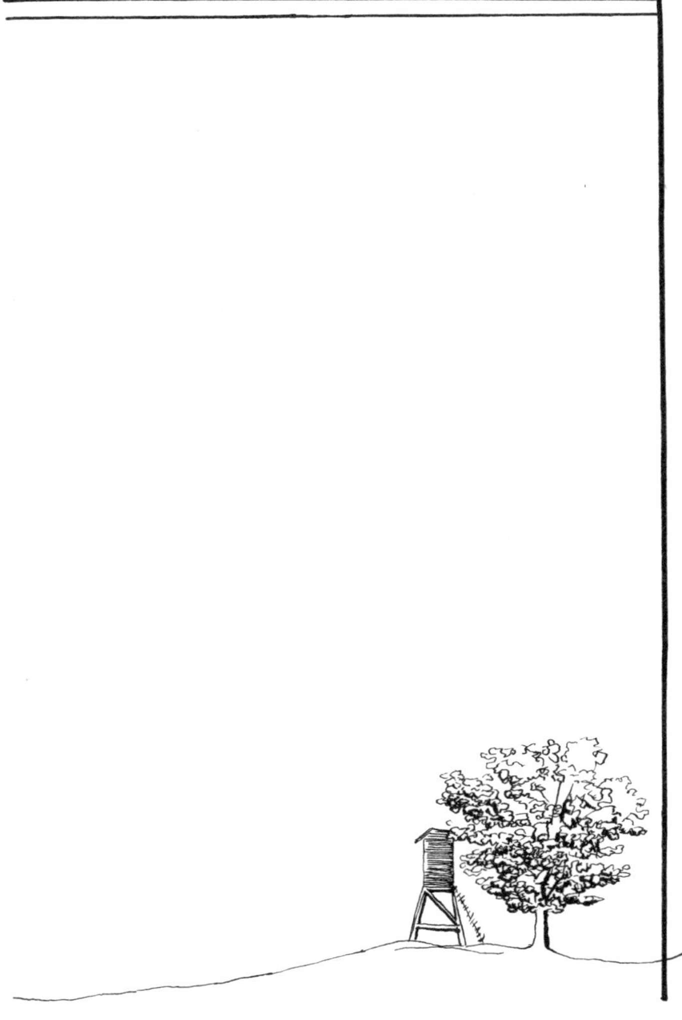

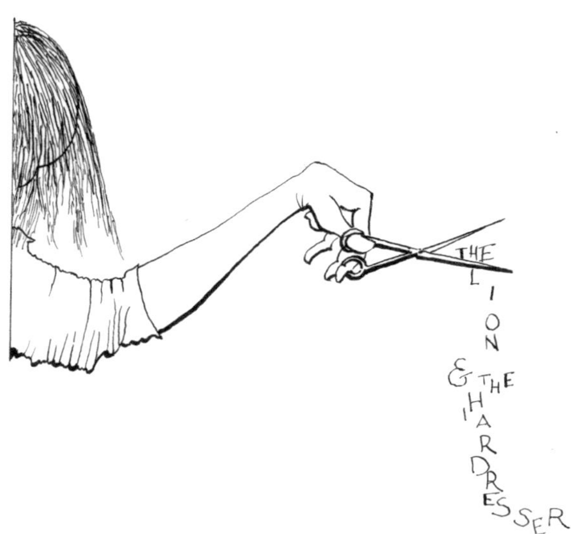
THE
LION
& THE
HAIRDRESSER

THE LION & THE HAIRDRESSER

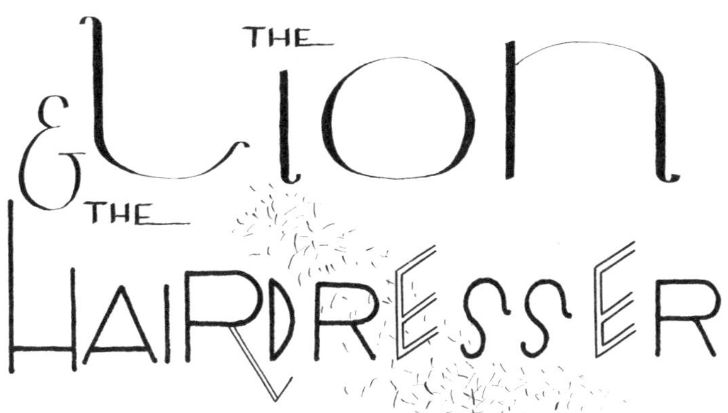

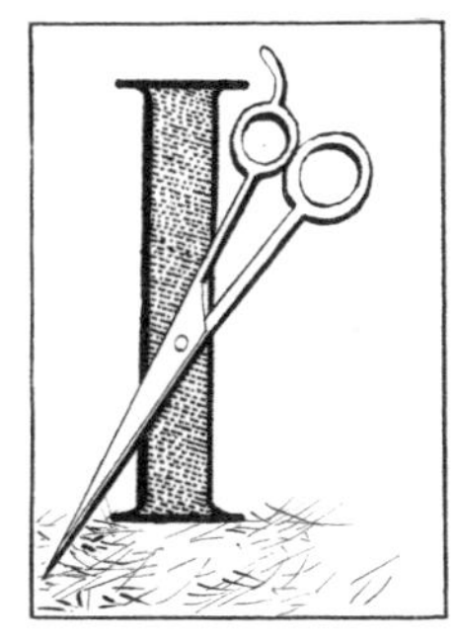

T WAS NOT YET commonly known, but rumours had begun to circulate among the animals in the kingdom that the Lion had reached the age when his powers would soon wane. Getting a whiff of this, the Lion sought ways to strengthen his public appearance and consulted one of his most faithful acquaintances: the Hairdresser.

Upon being summoned, the Hairdresser hurried to the Lion's lair and approached him with a humble bow that never failed to charm the Animal King. Indeed the barber's modesty

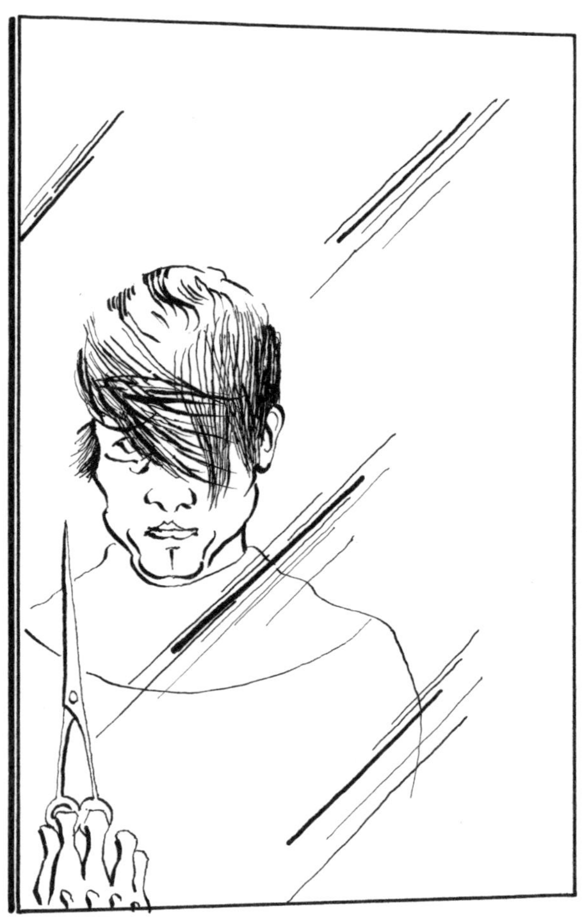

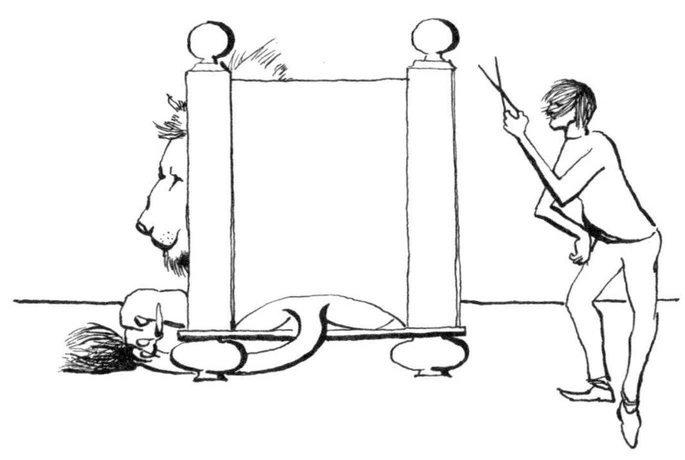

and genteel conversation had prevented the Lion from ever suspecting that it was nobody else but the Hairdresser who had started the rumour. For he knew that the weaker the Lion felt, the more the Animal King would cling to his advice. Unaware of these machinations, the Lion welcomed his subject:

"Loyal friend, I beseech thee, for my image is slipping and I seek your counsel."

On hearing this, the groom bowed once more and responded, "Your Majesty, your humble, faithful hairdresser ... at your service."

Soothed by the sound of these familiar words the Lion grew more candid and the Hairdresser saw the moment to advance his most daring proposition:

"A cut, your Majesty?" proposed the wily barber casually withdrawing his shears. And leaning close to the Lion's mighty head, whispered, "Grooming would do you well at this time, and why not rid yourself of that cumbersome mane..."

But something in the ring of these words let the cutter's motive slip.

The Lion's blood ran cold. He tore at his cloth, turned to the Hairdresser and roared, "A cut you say? Then cuts it shall be. No beast of any power shall retain a single hair save myself. Haircuts for the entire court! I decree! Severe haircuts! And when you are done, I will see to it that they turn upon you and your lanky locks."

• And so the Lion Kept Power •

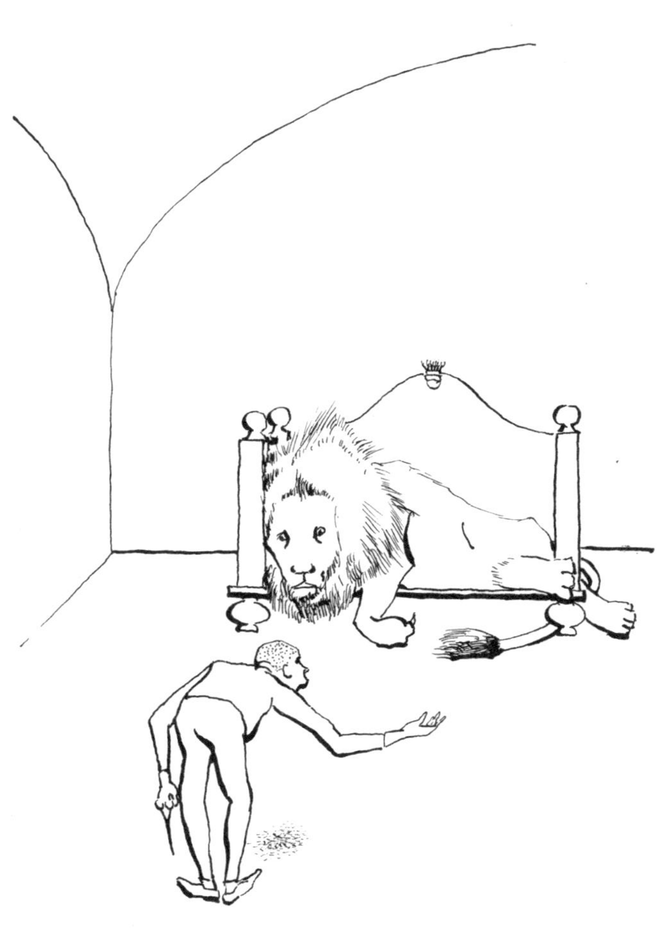

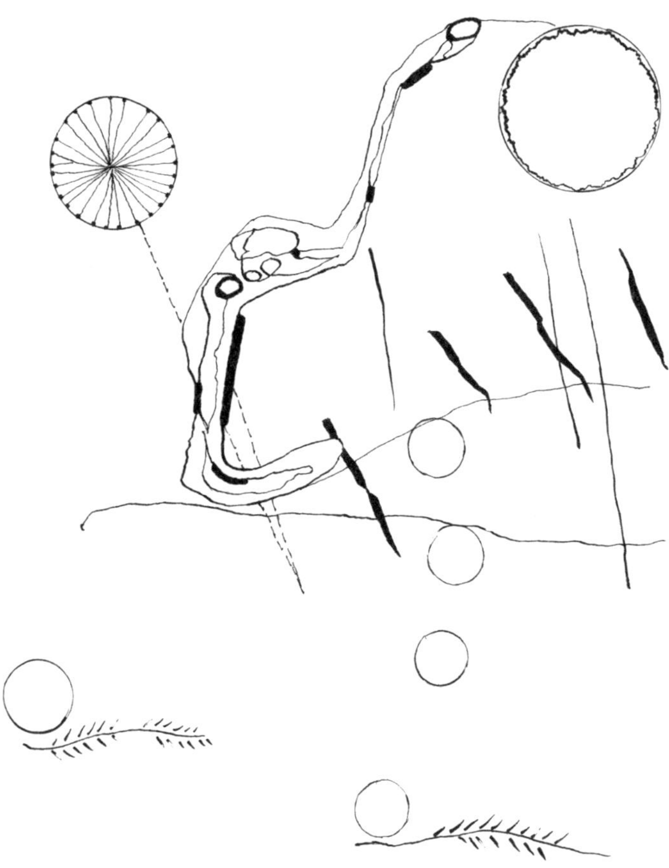

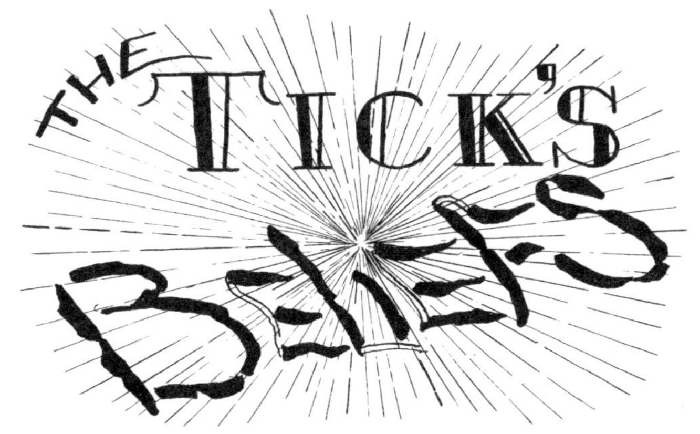

VI

H A!" CRIED THE TICK when it hopped on the Mare, and thought to itself, "What have we here? A Mare, how delicious!"

The Mare gasped as it felt the pinch of the Tick enter its flank.

"Who are you to take me so?" it anxiously inquired.

"I am your future," spoke the Tick. "To feed me is your vocation. Look at all that I have given up for you. The green grass. The rustling leaves. The comfort of the shady meadows. All this I sacrificed. Do not question my noble intentions!"

"So be it!" said the Mare. "My fate is sealed!" and resumed to graze peacefully.

And as the Tick engorged, a tiny organism, as small to it as it was to the Mare, wiggled from whence it feasted within the bloated tract inside the Tick.

"I am smaller than you and more noble by far," it said. "Feeding me is *your* obligation."

When it heard these words, the Tick brightened up and stated with great resolve. "How generous it is of me to recognise everyone's innermost desire! I enlightened the Mare of its true profession. Now I nourish a force within that abides by my very own convictions. Justice I thus do to the big and the small. What a wonderful creature I am!"

The Tick eventually died, consumed from within, yet at peace with the world at large.

A Quite Enviable Condition!

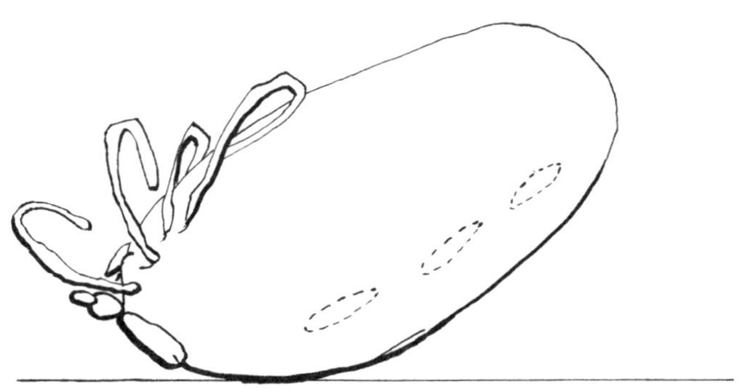

VII

THE ○ ANT ○ AND ○ THE

RECLINING BEAUTY

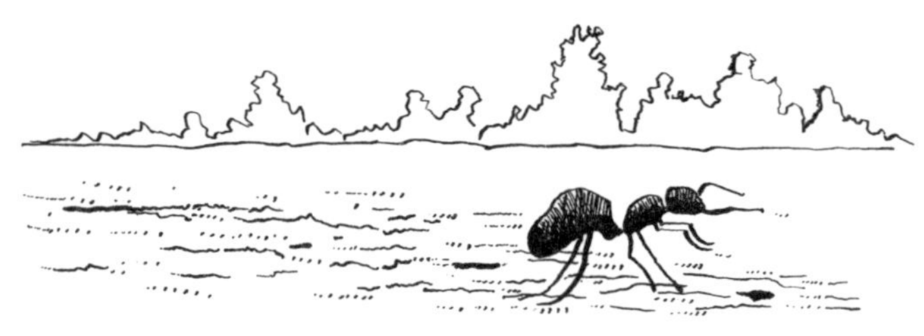

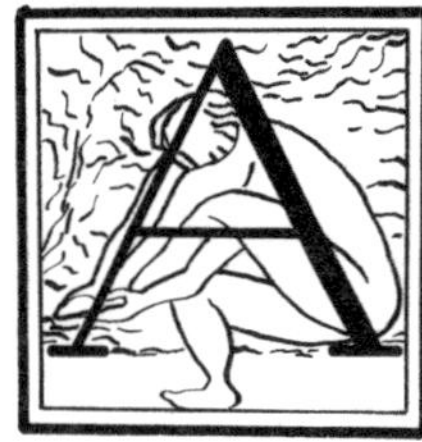

FTER a hard day's work, the Ant set out on his long way home. Spent and tired, he came upon a clearing where a figure was reclining on a podium.

"Life is unjust!" the Ant cried furiously at the figure. "I work so hard and all *you* do is lie out and enjoy the surroundings. And at the end of the day you never have to worry about getting home because you never move at all!"

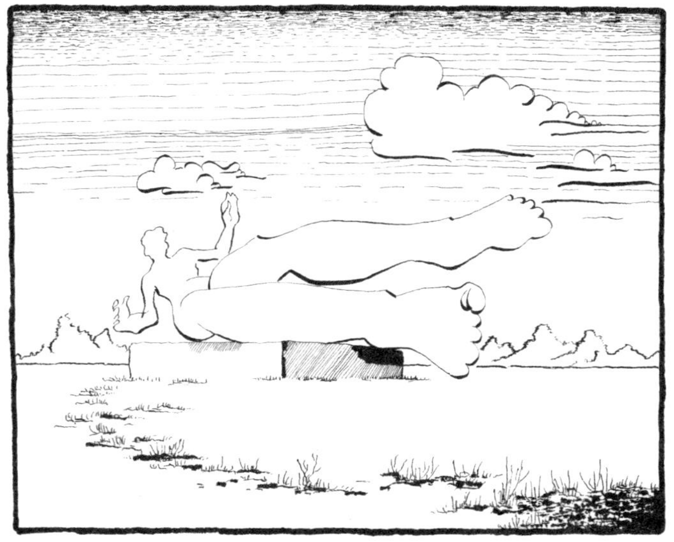

"Oh dear friend, don't do me wrong," the figure pleaded with the Ant. "Holding my position in harmony with these surroundings is such hard work. No one ever understands how strenuous it is. I would be so lucky if I could roam around in the woods and carry things like you do. Then the people would finally see what I could do!"

"This can easily be arranged," the Ant replied, and without a moment's hesitation he scrambled up the pedestal. "Get off and I will take your place!"

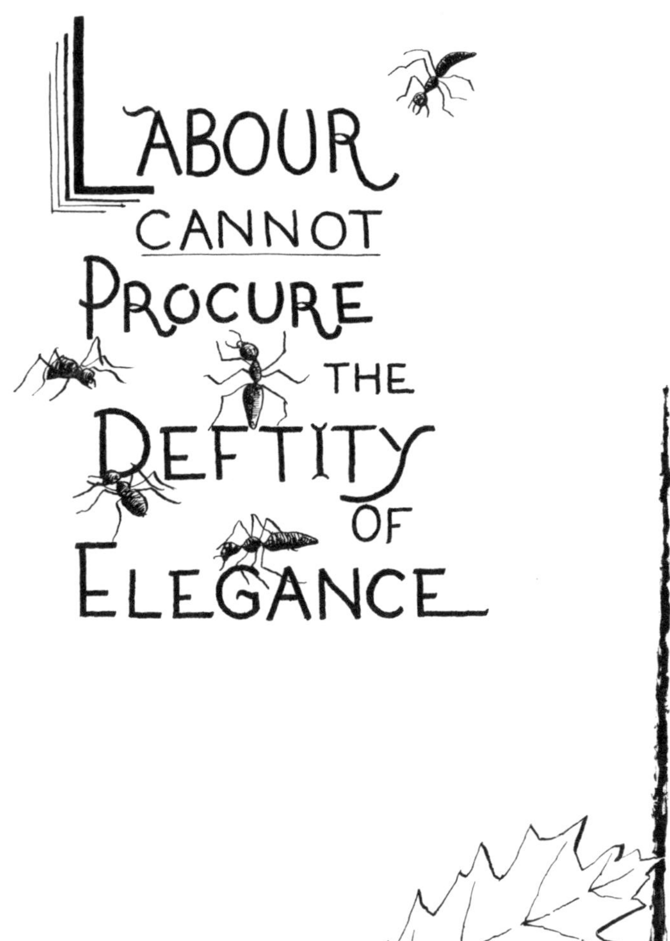
LABOUR
CANNOT
PROCURE
THE
DEFTITY
OF
ELEGANCE

Relieved for the chance to relax, the reclining figure willingly dismounted. The Ant then scurried around erratically on the podium moving fallen leaves back and forth.

"This will not do," said the figure of Beauty looking on disapprovingly. "Your toiling is in vain. You must now learn to be motionless, this is a far greater perfection."

Try as he might the Ant could not sit still.

"What are you looking at?" replied the Ant out of breath. "Make busy with your carrying!"

But unable to think of anything she could carry or otherwise do, the Beauty just stood transfixed, sad and silent.

Watching the scene from above, Jove held his belly laughing and exclaimed, "Hard labour will never procure what elegance yields without effort. But rarely do the idle live in peace with themselves for they know not how blessed they are!"

SELDOM
do the IDLE
LIVE in PEACE

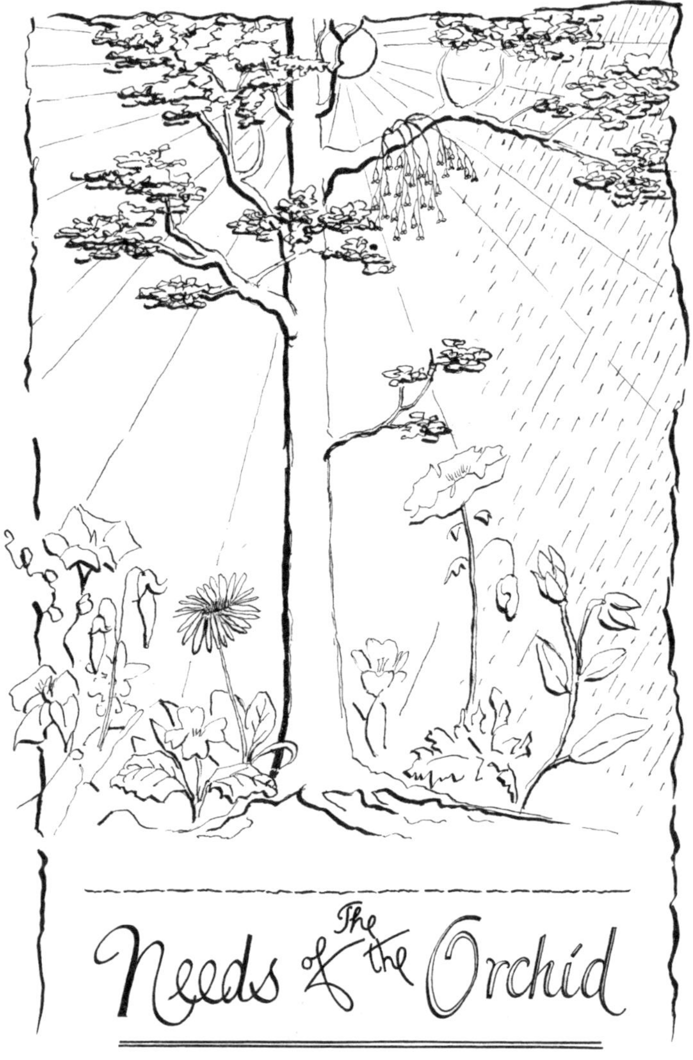

VIII

Needs of The Orchid

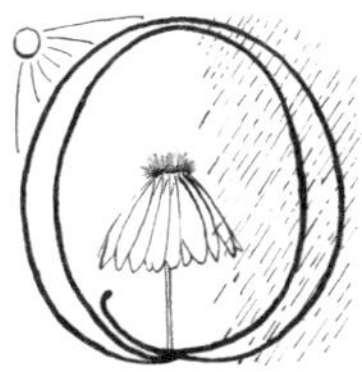O**F ALL THE FLOWERS** in the garden the Orchid is the most difficult to please. Gardeners try to no avail. The Orchid's heads remain droopy, and rarely utter a word. So how can one tell what the poor flower wants?

The silence of the Orchid weighs heavily on the souls of the other flowers. Over time they too stop speaking and drop their heads. Even the Cheery Daisies cease their chatter.

One day the silence of the flowers became so pervasive that even the Sun and the Rain started to feel glum.

"Listen!" the Sun said to the Rain. "To shine on the flowers gave me so much joy, but now that I can no longer lighten their mood, I see no sense in what I do. I can hardly muster the energy to rise in the morning!"

"Oh…" replied the Rain, "neither, drip drop, do I refresh them, so I, drip drop, don't see sense in, pitter-patter, persevering…"

"Enough!" decried the Sun, "let us resolve the origin of this foul mood!"

Not long into their search they came upon

the Orchid, pale of petal, hiding in the shadow of a large tree, perching on bough.

"What, pray tell are you lacking?" the direct Sun enquired. "Since frankly, nothing we offer makes the slightest bit of difference. Lift your heads and see how your discontent spreads!"

But alas, the petulant flower was in no mood to converse.

"I am entitled to all I touch," was the Orchid's only response.

"Such arrogance!" exclaimed the Sun storming off.

The gentle Rain persisted a little longer... and then its drips ceased to fall.

Without sun and rain how can a garden grow?

It cannot.

The flowers die.

All but one that is.

One that needs neither water nor light. It lives off another. Even when there is only rot left to feed on. It's the Orchid – absorbed in its own woes.

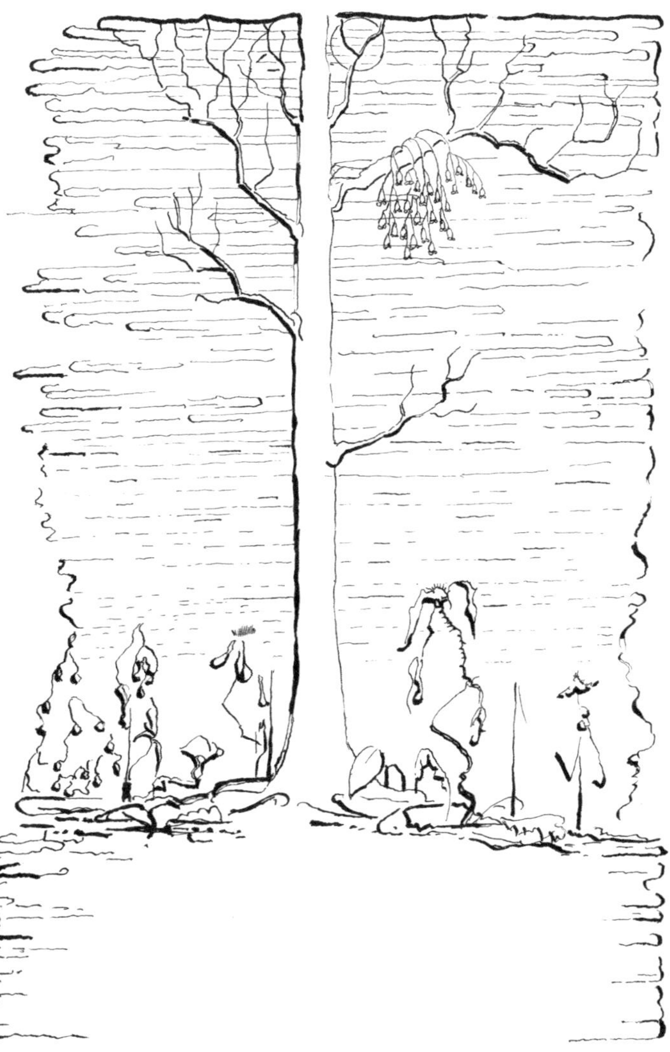

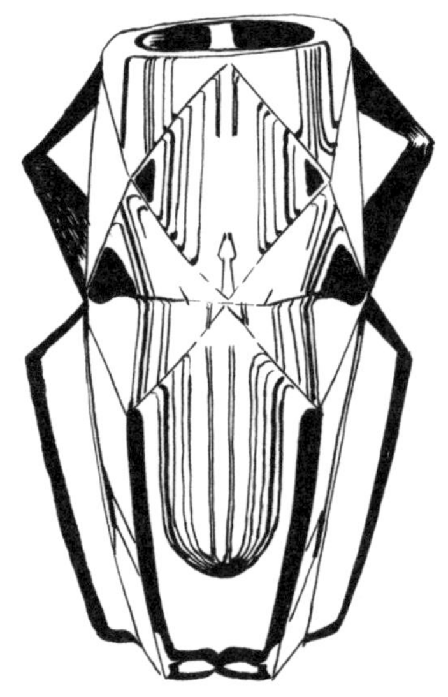

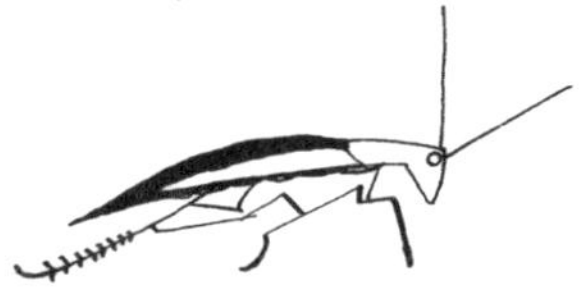

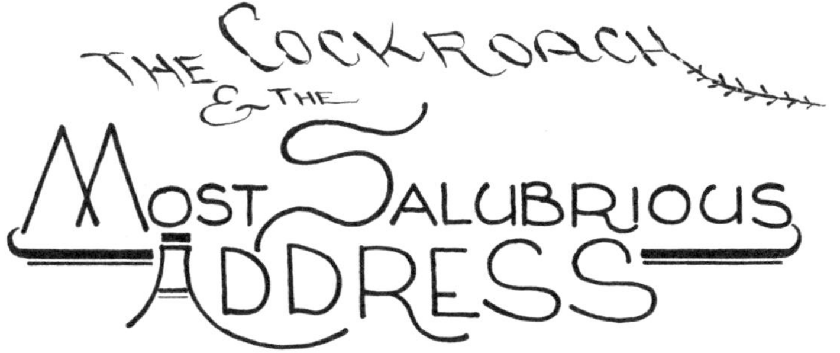

IX

THE COCKROACH & THE MOST SALUBRIOUS ADDRESS

ON THE LOOK for new digs the Cockroach happened upon a stately manor. It was the Most Salubrious Address.

With a grin it chimed, "If the house makes the Roach, then here I live my days," and crawled inside.

The Most Salubrious Address, a much-refined character, did not notice this at first but being sensitive soon discerned a certain unsavoury odour. Choking on the very thought, it grabbed the snuffbox and inhaled until respectability was restored.

Sometime later while cleaning, the Address heard a hiss from behind the crystal glass collection. Eventually the Roach appeared in full view, sauntering out from behind a fine piece of Baccarat stemware. "Pestilence!" screamed the Address, mortified at what crept before its eyes. "It is the walking unwashed."

"Ah, my friend…" sighed the Roach, "what's the rumpus? Why would a manor like you be averse to the joys of cohabitation? Now that you've been on the market for so long, I reckon you could do with some company!"

"Vermin! Don't you see, in the company of your kind, my price will fall and fall further every day!" cried the Address.

"The price perhaps…" smiled the Roach, "but in our company the number of us who know the *value* of living with you will rise and rise indefinitely, by the hour!"

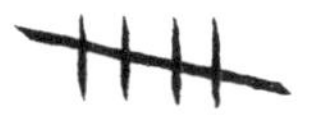

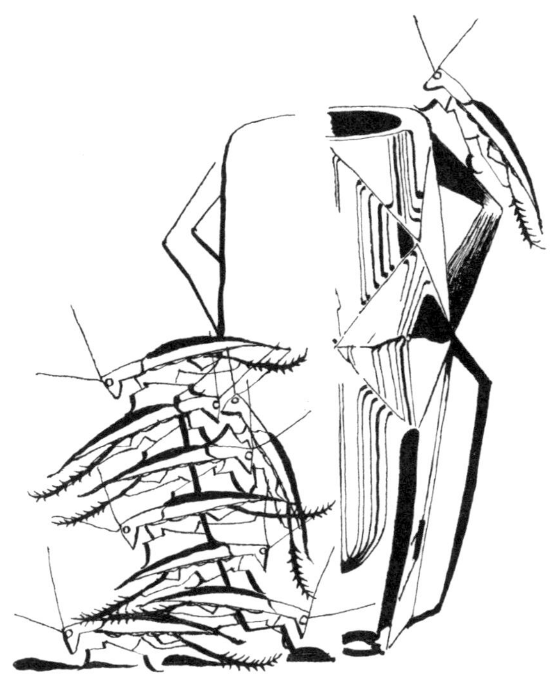

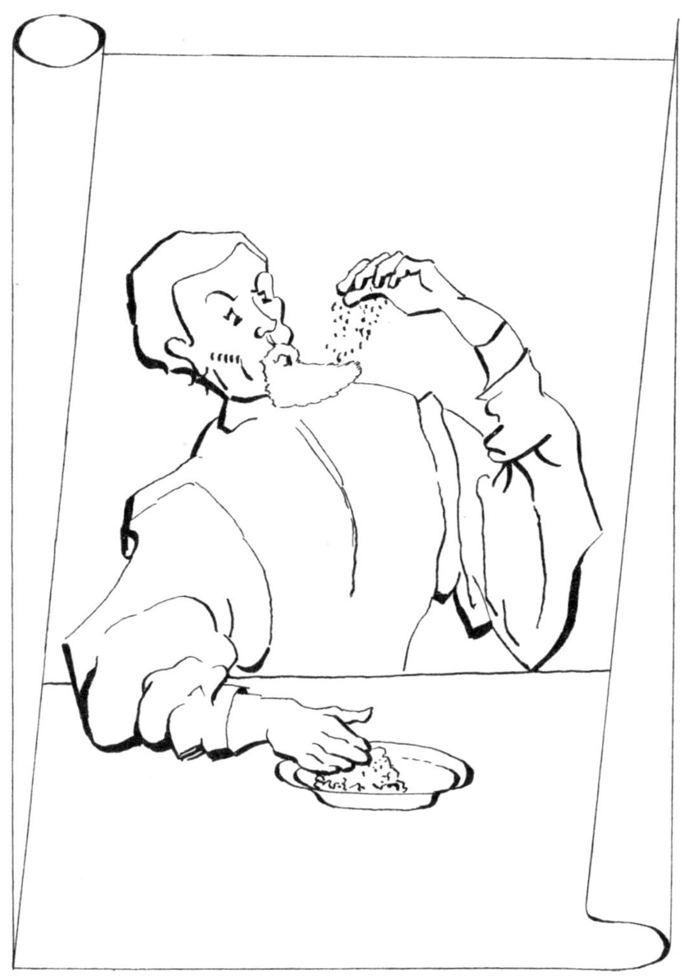

THE MOCK LUNCHTIME BEARD

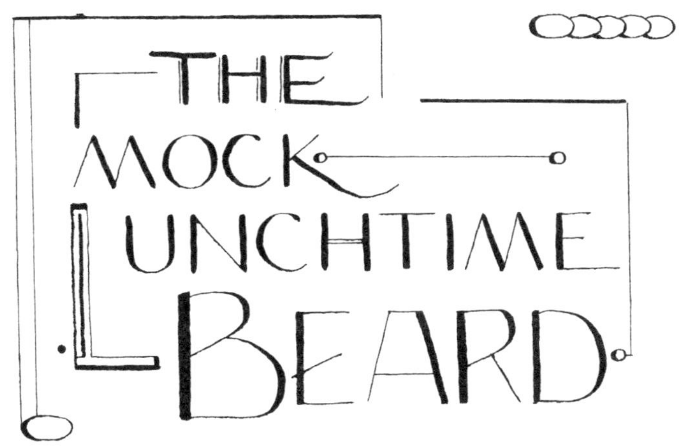

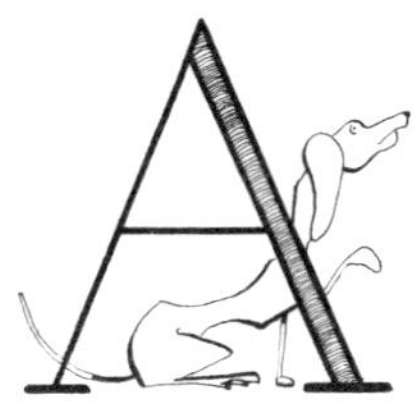A NOBLE MAN who was thought to be rich but had actually fallen on hard times spent much of his day defending his honour.

He sat in his still, grand house with his faithful Hound without a scrap to eat! At lunchtime, as the Hound watched, the Noble Man would gather crumbs of bread and sprinkle them in his beard. After which he would walk through the streets, parading his Mock Lunchtime Beard.

And the people who saw the sight thought to themselves, "There goes a man who still lunches well!"

Loyal to its master and ready to accommodate any of his whims, the Hound turned a blind eye to all future ramifications of his behaviour, and even took care of providing a steady supply of dried bread found in neighbours' scrap heaps. Loyalty forbade the Hound to question that, while supplying bread for sprinkles, it had not been fed for weeks! It didn't even protest when its master, looking at the Hound's emancipated figure, decided it was no longer fit to be seen on the streets.

Little is known of what became of the Noble Man. There was no one to tell the tale, as the most intimate witness to his fate, the Hound, withered away before him, faithful to the end.

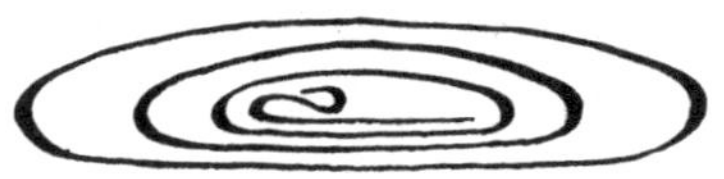

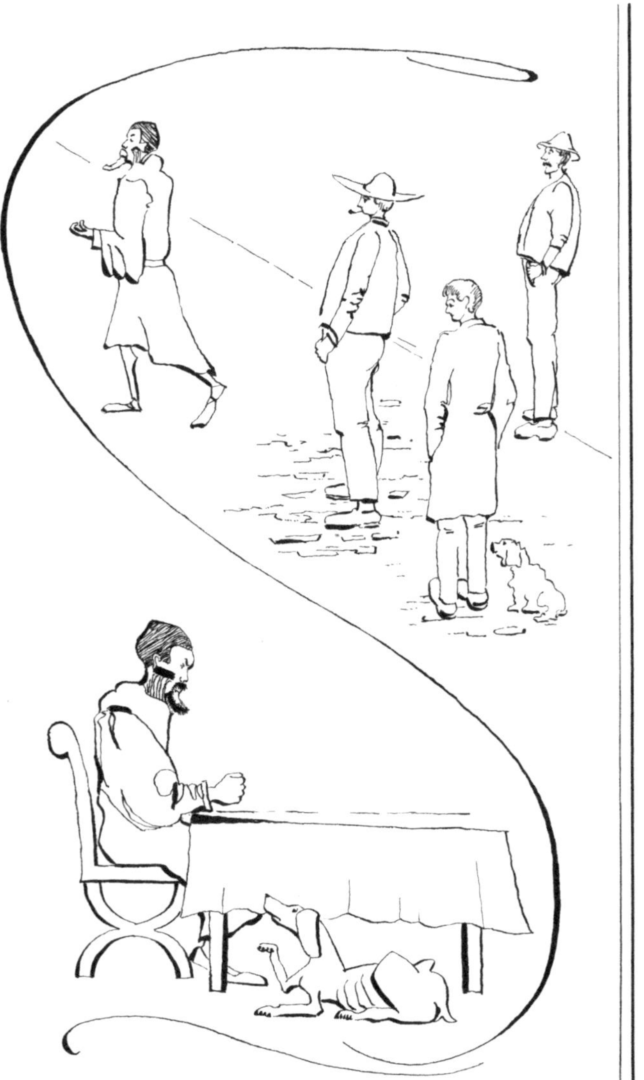

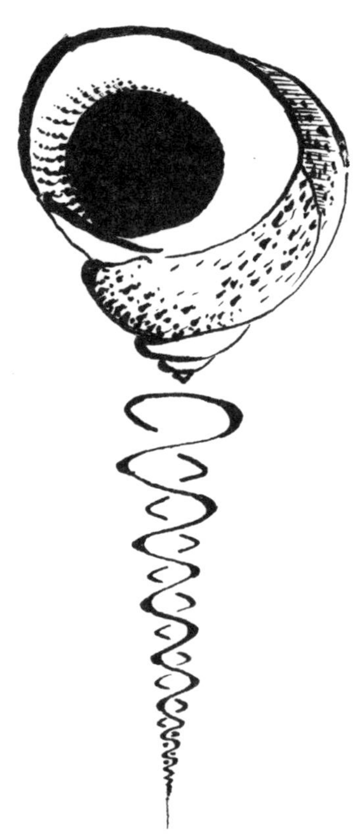

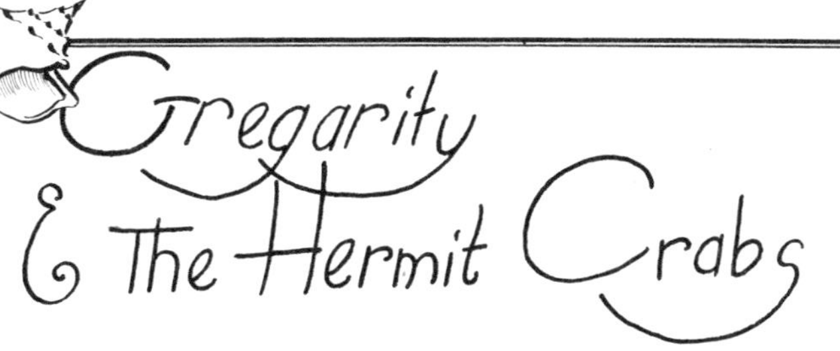 Gregarity & The Hermit Crabs

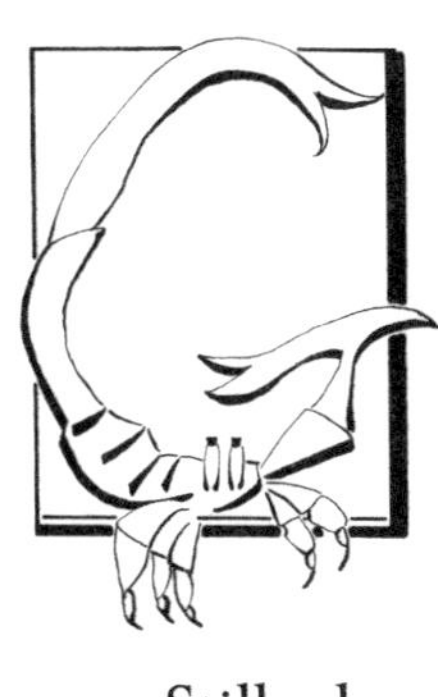

REGARITY HAD LOST her faith in the world. She has seen too many disheartening acts committed by the earth's creatures that it had become hard to believe in their talent for convivial living. Sad she thus turned, very sad.

Still, she continued to travel the lands and seas in the faint hope of once again finding a species that knew the joys of communal life.

On her voyage she met the Hermit Crabs, and in their habit of seeking residence in deserted seashells she saw her grim outlook confirmed.

"Oh what unsociable beasts you are!" Gregarity snapped. "Not only do you shy away from traversing the open waters where fish mix and mingle freely, what's worse is that you have no qualms about retreating into the ruins of another being's existence!"

"Dear Gregarity," the Ombudscrab kindly spoke, "Word is out that lately you seem rather glum. Please permit me to invite you for a stroll through our colony. Who knows, maybe we can raise your spirits?"

Wallowing in her misery Gregarity replied, "Wretchedness, that I am left with your puny, misanthropic race! Is there not one empathic soul left in this world? Are we all alone? Must we employ competition as the only law of nature?"

As she spoke she heard the young Crabs convening.

"Join us please," implored the Ombudscrab. "The sun is going down, we are about to eat and enjoy the pleasures of this evening together."

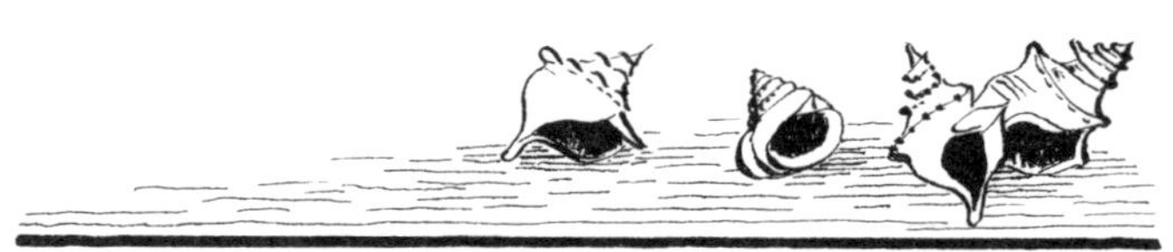

And so, with nothing else to lose, Gregarity waded in.

She was greeted by a lively bunch, each with shell, robust in conversation on the only subject of interest: real estate! There were Crabs set on leaving shells for bigger shells, and smaller Crabs intent on taking up the soon-to-be vacated units. There was scurrying, exchanging and chirping, all in good camaraderie, and without a pause even during dinner! Their table manners were appalling, but Gregarity saw no malice as they shared both food and lodgings, the stuff of life, together in solidarity.

A smile spread over her face and Gregarity sensed once more her faith in the world.

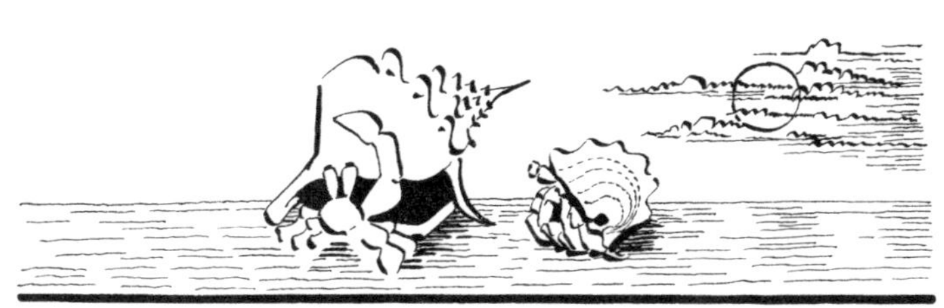

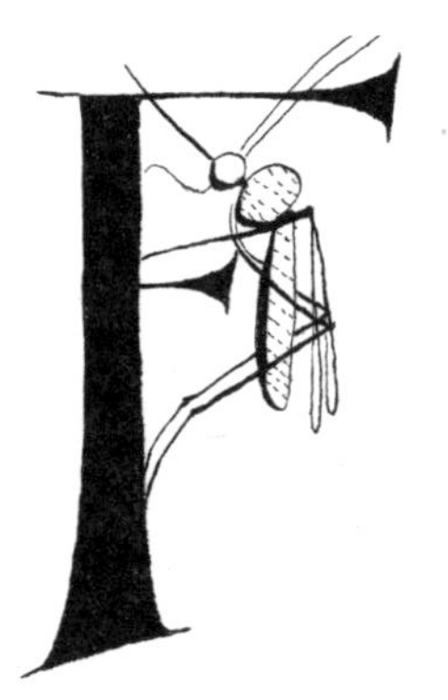

THE MOSQUITO

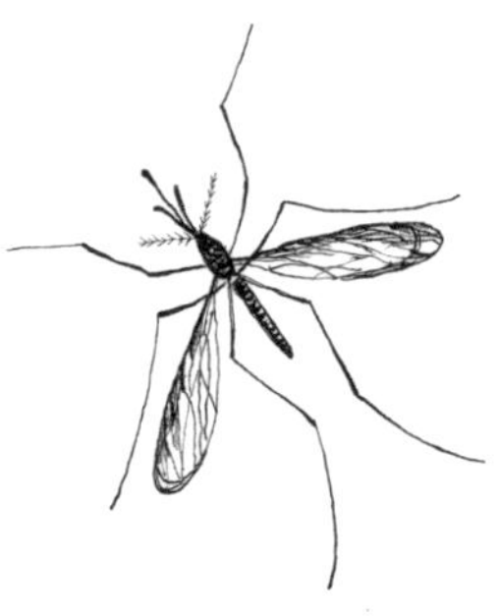

FOR AS LONG as she could remember, the Mosquito had been feeling an anger build inside her. Growing stronger every day, her buzz acquired a peculiarly penetrating pitch. One day when she could bear it no longer, the Mosquito addressed the People of France.

"You! People of the first Republic! You have talked to me of culture, reason, and

XII

THE PEOPLE of FRANCE

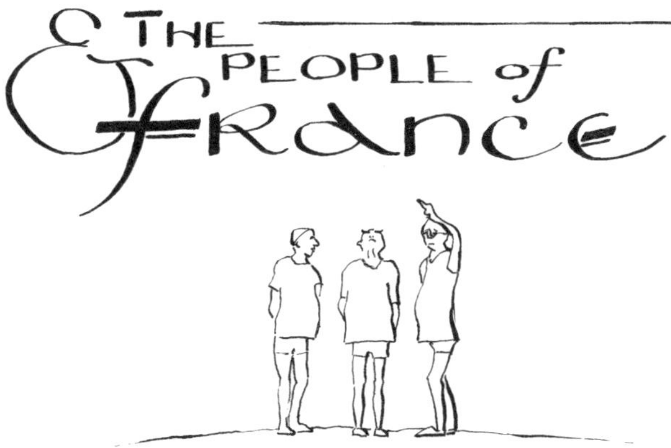

refinement, but never, I repeat, Bzzzzzzzzzz, never has any one of your great accomplishments made a drop of your blood taste any more wholesome! Bzzzzzzzzzz. What are the triumphs of civilization worth when its fruits cannot satisfy the appetite of a simple creature like me?! All I ask for is satisfaction... Bzzzzzzzzzzz."

Rising up, the People of France formulated their defense:

"We are the People of France, and we are civilized! When accusations are levelled... there is due process. Firstly... all we ask is that you be reasonable, abide by the standards of conduct, and refrain from this incessant buzzing!"

Only more incensed by the People's address, the Mosquito refrained with new vigour.

"All I ask for is satisfaction!... BZZZZZZ..."

"The People of France do not judge by relative size, however, we do find your attitude exceedingly small-minded. We are a sanguine breed and we never take kindly to interlopers. CEASE YOUR BUZZING NOW!"

That was enough. The Mosquito, seeing red, released her most piercing refrain:

"SATISFACTION!... BZZZZZZZZZZ..."

Then, sixty-five million arms in unison hurled an avalanche of weighty tomes that struck squarely upon the Mosquito's head. The thundering resonance was heard half a world away. Thus the People of France settled their dispute with the recalcitrant Mosquito.

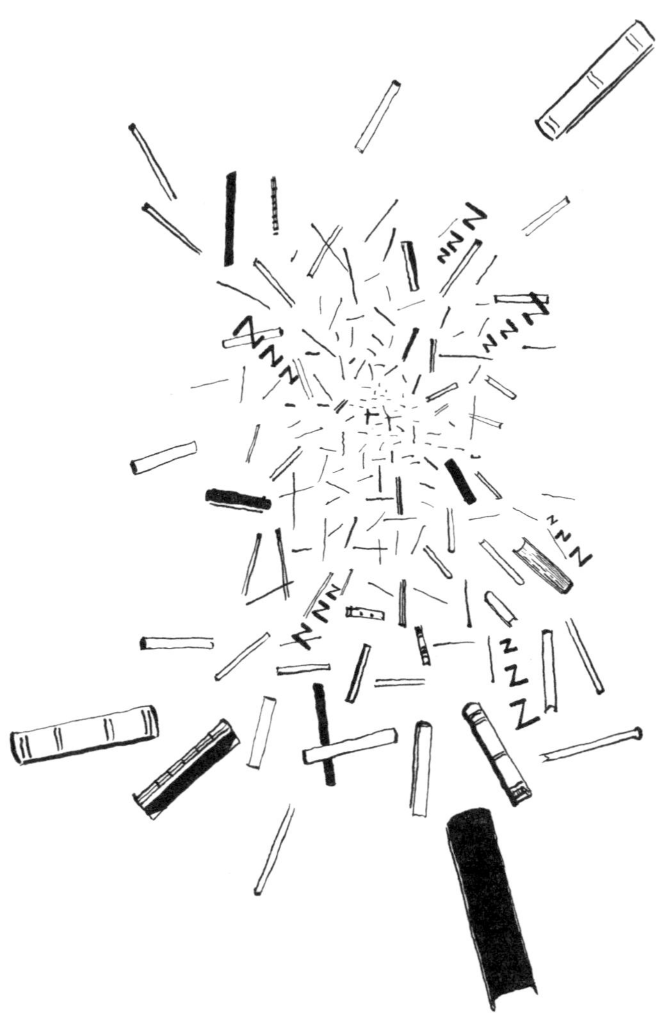

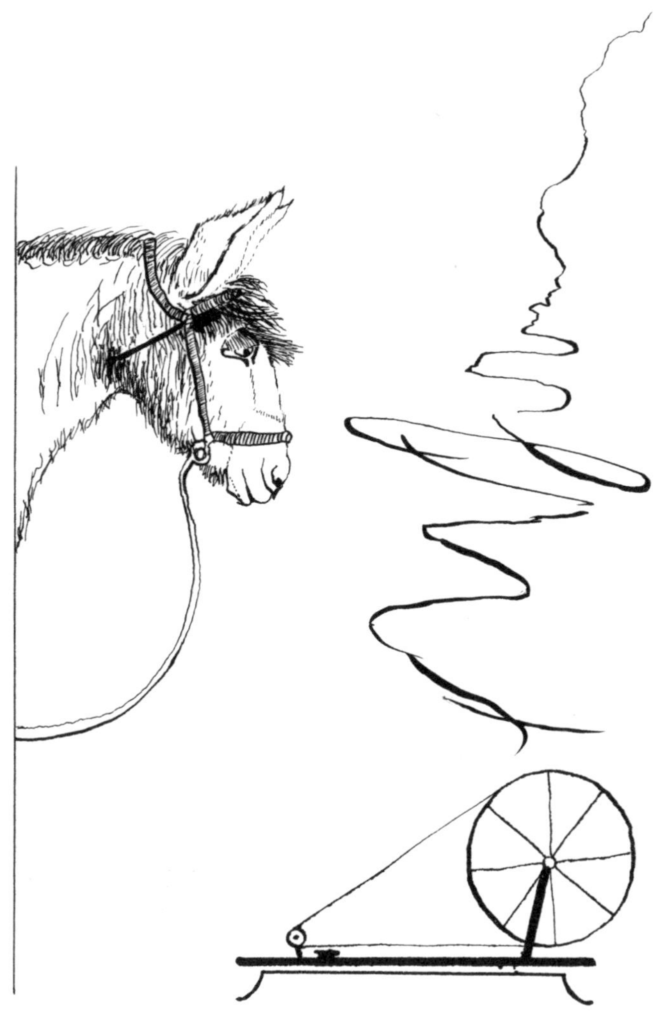

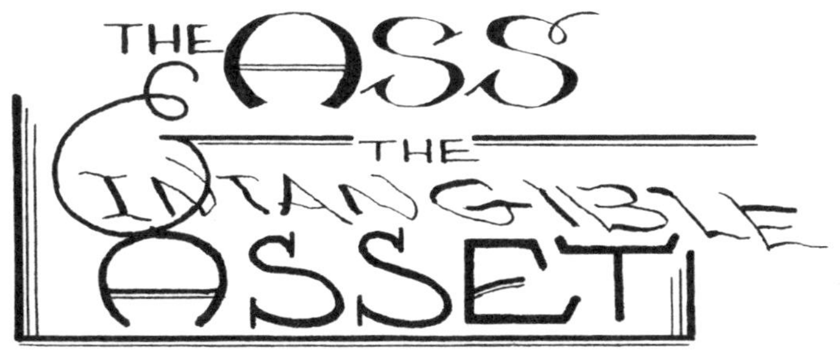

XIII

*Who turns the great wheel and for whom
does the great wheel turn?*

*Who wills its engines and, after a day's
work, what conversations would be had?*

WHEN THE ASS met the Intangible Asset it said, "How do you do?"

Whereupon the Asset shot back, "What kind of question is this? I'm not at liberty to reveal my disposition to just any inquisitive ass. What I am, and what state I'm in, is a secret my owners ardently protect!"

"Easy now!" replied the Ass, "just trying to be polite. Me, I like a pat on the back after a hard day turning the beam in the mill, so I was thinking…"

"Hear hear! The Ass is thinking!" the Intangible Asset sneered. "But you know nought of what you speak. My labour does not end when the day is over, for I am potential. I am to be harboured at all times, be it day or night!"

"Oh, I see," the Ass said, "so… you don't get to rest, do you?"

"My simple friend," returned the Asset in an accomplished tone, "if you only knew with whom you were speaking. Discerning creatures far and wide can see my strength."

"Could you then," asked the Ass with open curiosity "turn this wheel?" Incensed, the Asset grabbed the beam and pushed. And it pushed and pushed and the wheel turned, indeed, faster and faster until the Intangible Asset melted away and there was nothing left, not a trace.

"That was quick," observed the Ass, and he shut down the mill for the day and went home to rest.

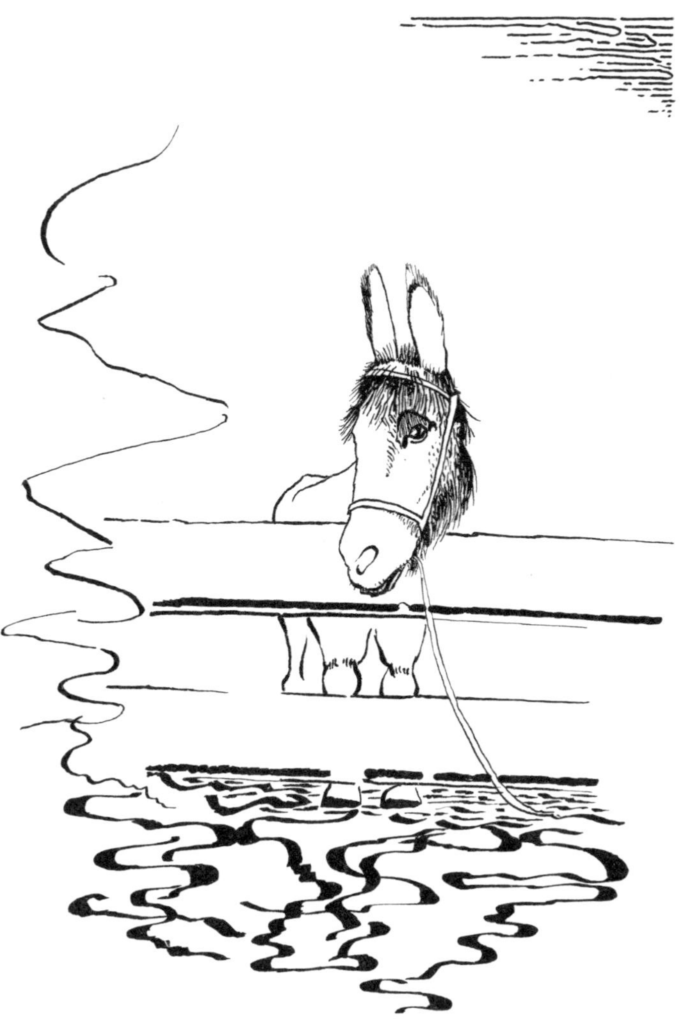

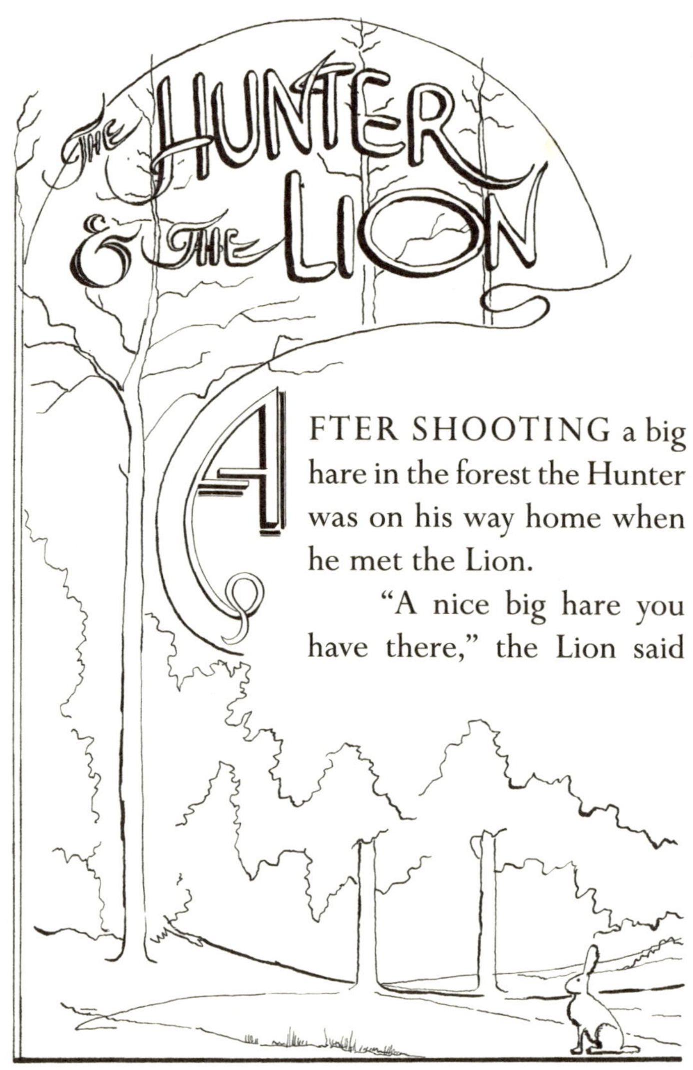

XIV

AFTER SHOOTING a big hare in the forest the Hunter was on his way home when he met the Lion.

"A nice big hare you have there," the Lion said

to the Hunter. "I am already looking forward to having my share of it for supper."

"So why would you think you could have a share of what I caught after a long day of hard work?" bellowed the Hunter in defiance.

"Well, you see," the Lion replied calmly, "the forest is mine just like it is yours. So I thought, letting you have half of what is mine was a fair offer. But if you protest, I will take it back and think of something new. How would you like to join the hare for supper then?"

Not quite realising the danger he was in, the Hunter took up the Lion's offer. At the Lion's lair he skilfully prepared the hare and served a splendid supper.

"I have never tasted such a delicious morsel," declared the Lion licking his chops. "Tell me your secret so I too can make this dish." And then, forgetting his earlier intentions he added, "Oblige me with your recipe and then please join me in this delectable supper."

The Hunter obliged and they dined together on the succulent meat.

A number of years pass and the Hunter has

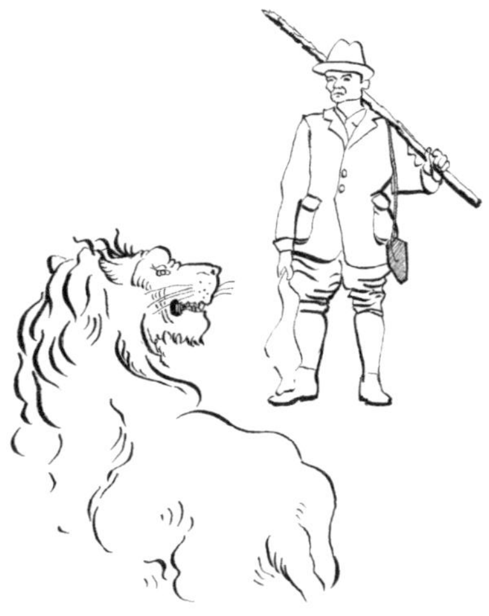

grown old. No matter how hard he tries, he fails to catch hares as easily as he used to.

"I have always been able to make a good living from selling my game but now I cannot even catch enough food to feed myself," said the Hunter. And then he remembered the Lion.

That evening in desperation he made his way to the Lion's lair. From a distance he could smell the aroma of hare, prepared just the way he had instructed. The Hunter's hunger overcame him. He burst in on the Lion and asked for a portion of the meal.

Seeing how famished his visitor was, the Lion roared with laughter.

"Now look what became of him who once ruled the forest, a cook who returns hungry to the kitchen!"

Full of shame the Hunter replied, "Your powers have outlasted my skills, but deride me not because I have shared with you all that I once had."

"True," the Lion returned, "but don't you see that I cannot return to you what I still possess. You gave me knowledge, and it is beyond me to give your power back to you. Stay in my lair if you wish. But a hunter you will be no more."

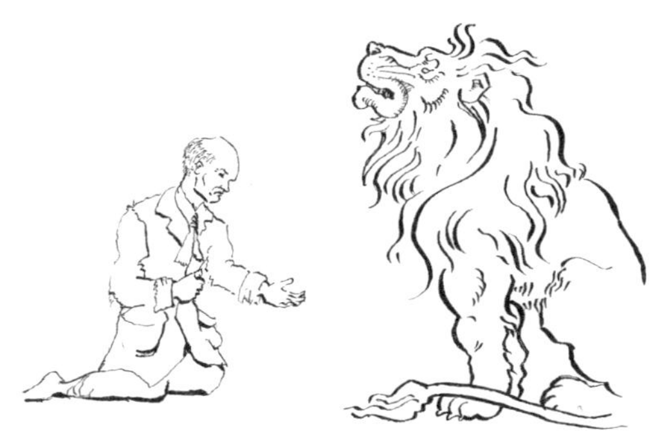

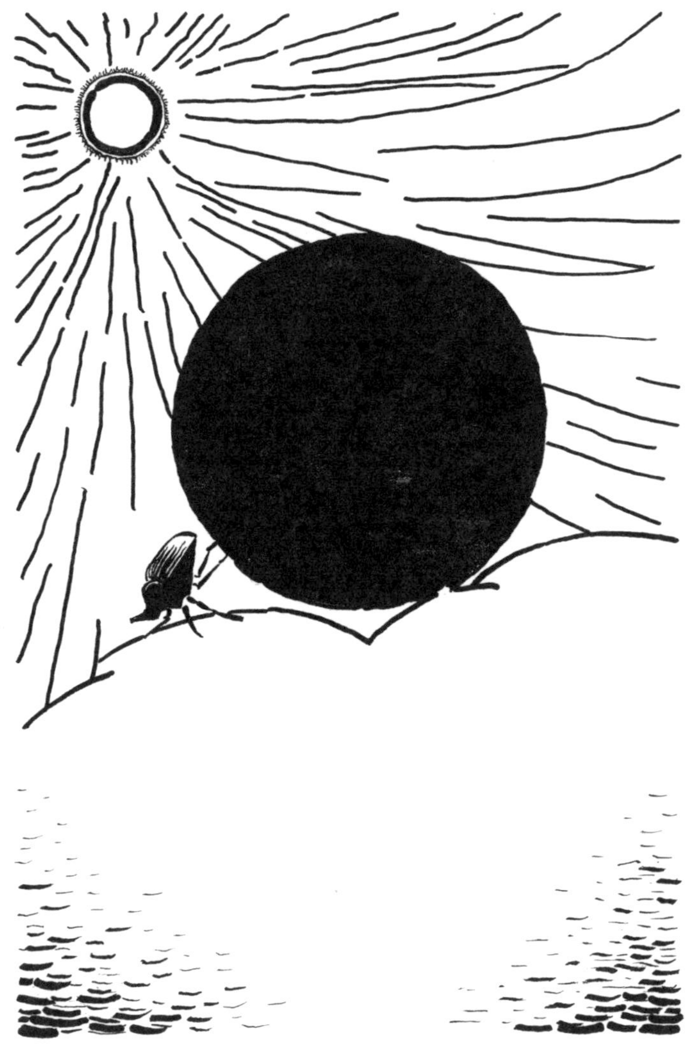

THE · DUNG · BEETLE
AND
THE · ORDURE · BALL

NDER THE HEAT of a noonday sun the Dung Beetle toiled, with patience and devotion, pushing the Ordure Ball up hill. Hind in the air, it scurried with nothing more than a view to the ground; and the Ball rolling, rolling ever upward, steadily growing and becoming more shapely. Having finally managed the incline, the Beetle clambered on top of the Ball to enjoy the scene. The Ball, round, full, and giddy from rolling, felt the inertia of the descending landscape.

And that was when the penny dropped. The Ball knew the time was ripe.

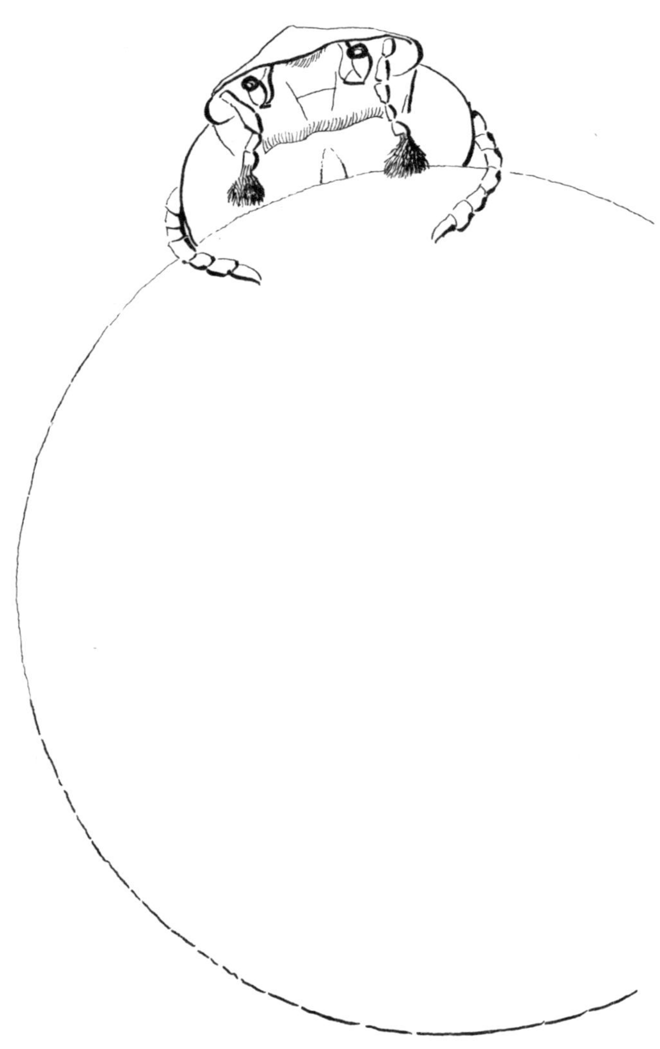

"I *will* rid myself of this petty Beetle. It has pushed me around for too long. I want this bug off my back!" it proclaimed defiantly. "A Ball of my dimension deserves choice in where to go and what to roll over. As far as the eye can see, the land lies ready for me to wallow in its mud, where and whenever I want."

The Beetle sensed that something was amok and clambered down from the stirring Ball.

"Another one too full of itself, oh well..." it said resigned, and scurried off to start afresh, leaving the deluded Ball to compost.

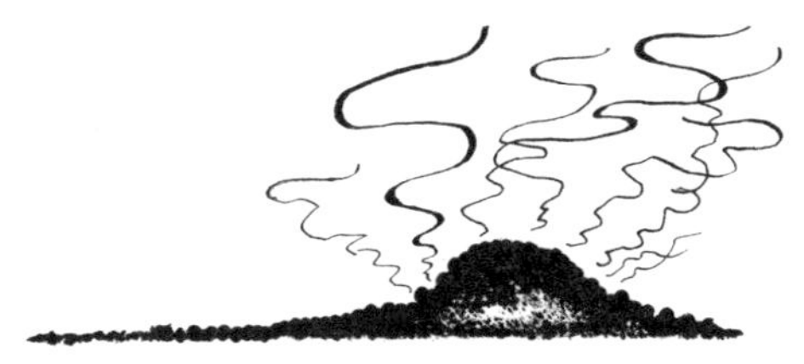

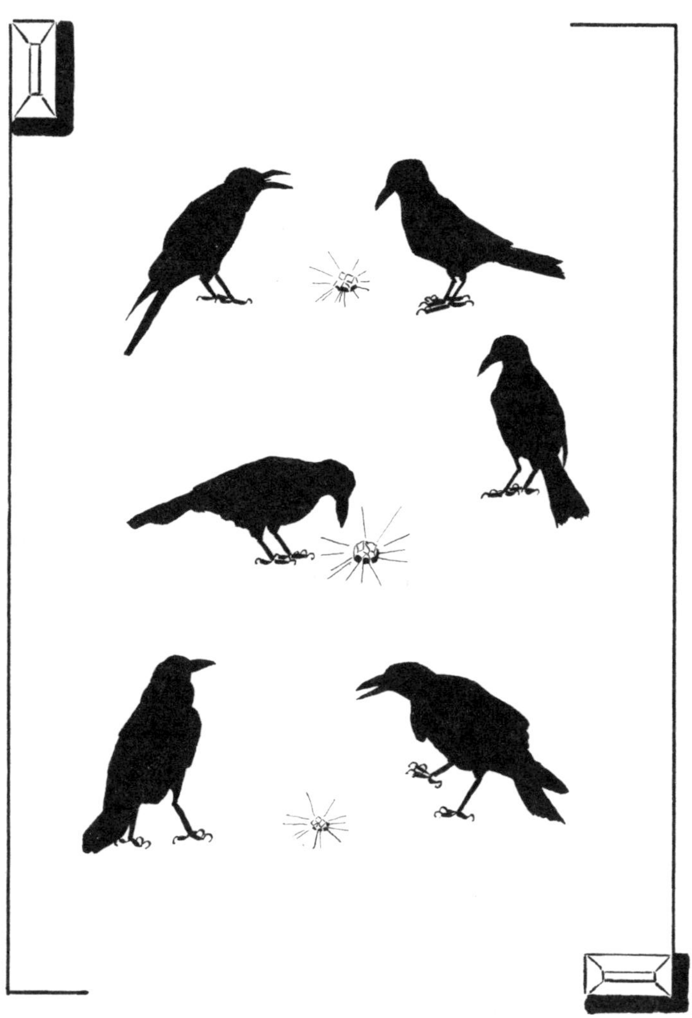

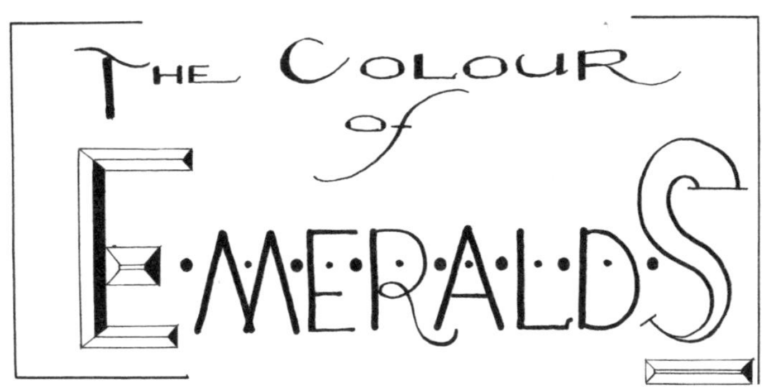

XVI

The Colour of Emeralds

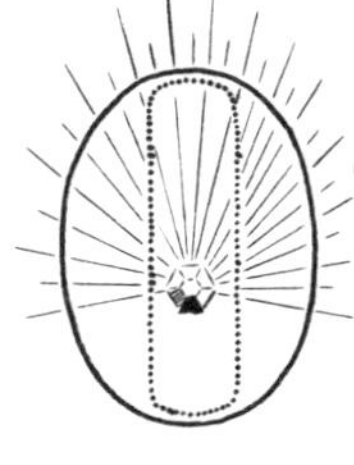

ON A HOT DUSTY ROAD in the morning sun a hoard of black ravens gathered around a small glistening stone. The birds, ruffled of feather, were attempting to settle a dispute…

The first bird, Raven A insisted the stone was an Emerald because it appeared to be green, and asked the others if they had ever seen an Emerald that was not green.

Raven B concurred, stating that from its usual vantage, in a tree outside the local jeweller's window, all Emeralds observed were green, therefore this green stone was indeed an Emerald.

C observed the stone as more blue-ish than green-ish, adding that it was perhaps just cut glass.

A shot back, "If that stone is not green, my feathers are not black, and neither are yours!"

With that, there was a noisy outburst and the banter continued well into the afternoon. As the sun inclined, there came a new observation. The stone now could only be described as blue.

"Eureka!" squawked C.

"Unsubstantiated, implausible, and utterly absurd," screeched A. "If green is blue, I am not black."

"Wait!" cried B. "You say if this is blue, you are not black. But blue it is and black you are. Therefore you lie!"

Betrayed by its plumage, A was set upon by the other Ravens. They fought and fought all night until the morning sun again found them, ruffled of feather, gathered around a small glistening stone, attempting to settle a dispute...

● ● ●

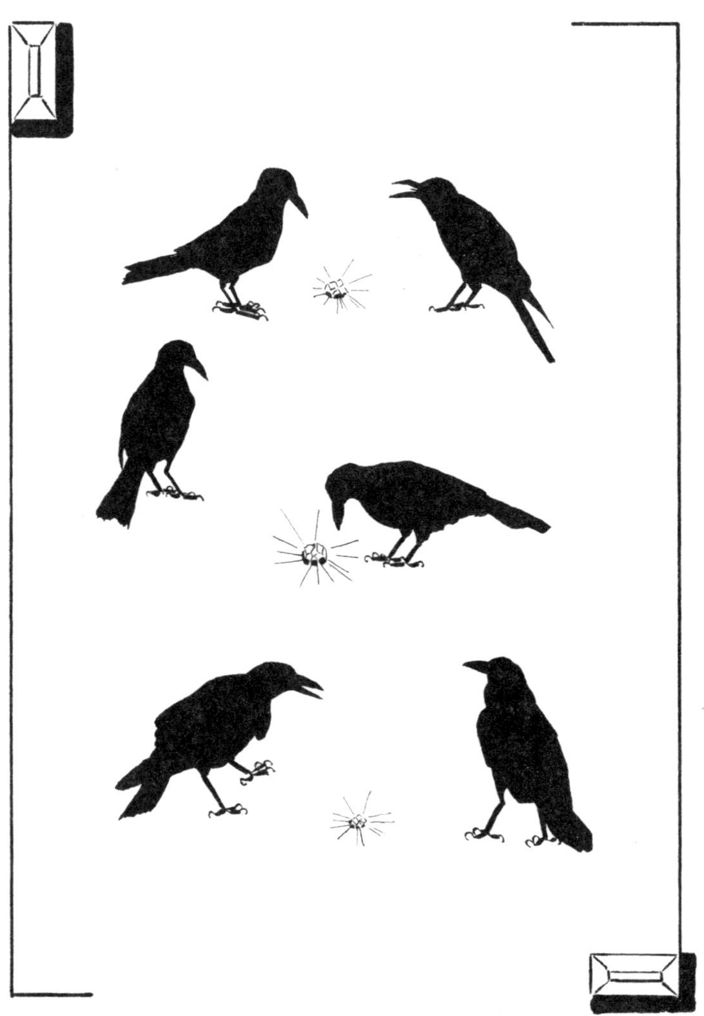

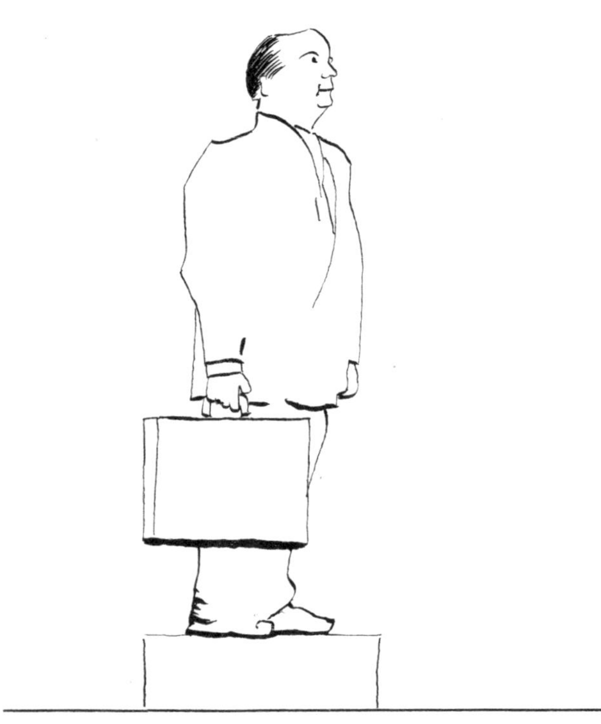

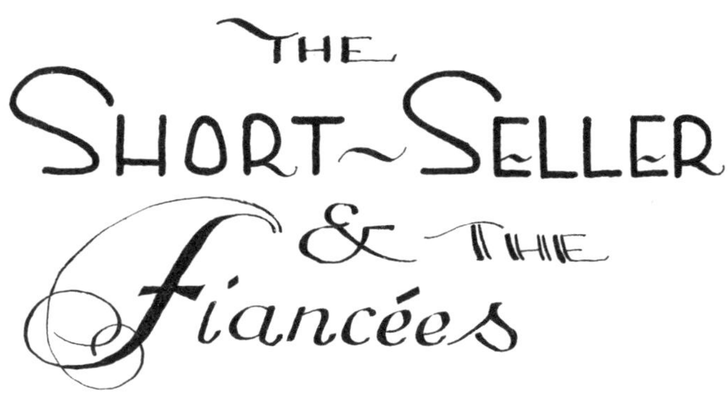

THE SHORT~SELLER & THE Fiancées

"NOT A MOMENT TO LOSE!" yelled the Short Seller to the Fiancées, perspiring profusely. "Bonds that go up can go down in a second. Reconsider your options! Hedge your bets! No shame in the game!"

Taken aback by this forceful address, the Fiancées exchanged nervous glances. For he felt, and she knew, that when signing the prenuptials each had been in doubt: what if, after sealing their bonds, the prospect arose to be with someone else, who was more fun and held higher status? Should we make good on existing contracts when better options still abound?

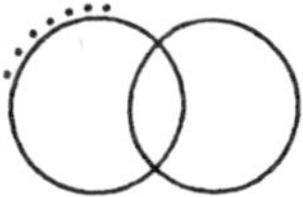

Aversion to such risk saw the betrothed furtively taking stock, followed by a brief sale of miscellaneous assets. They gave the cat away, knowing that if their bond was annulled, they would waste too much time fighting over who got to keep it. And who could blame them for taking preventative care on future potential losses?

"That's right!" the Short Seller cried. "If you take yourself out, you must put something back into the market. And in any case, if demands change, I can get you cats in a flash!"

Yet, later that day, he too felt doubt and was seen, only seconds before the closing bell struck, liaising with an insurance broker.

As evening settled on the exchange and the sounds of business faded, a hum remained, or rather more of a whisper. The voice of Doubt incarnate: "... rapid deals, life-long commerce, bonds quickly sealed and shortly sold on, in all there is me ... for I am the if, the would have, could have, should have, might have or might never be ... You may choose to hold on or pass off what may or may not be your fortune, but one thing you can be rest assured of, the enduring force behind all that you do will be me, the voice of the uncertain ..."

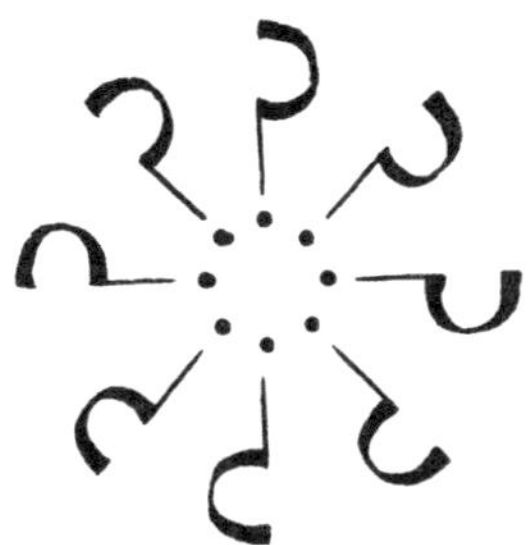

The Slug & the Vacancy Chain

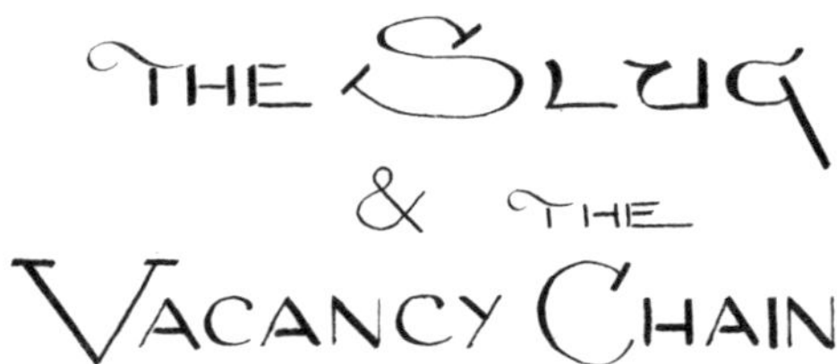

"AWFULLY SORRY to impinge on your time," said the Slug to the Vacancy Chain, "but I was told that you might have spare slots for those with no shell to carry, and thus are on the move..."

"Then move already!" the Chain shot back, leaving the Slug wondering, "But wait, where to?"

"To the next, to the next," called out the Chain. "No matter what, keep moving. Get a slot? Vacate it tomorrow! Roll up, roll up, and find another. Hesitate? There are others who won't. I could have another slug in a minute, so don't you ever, even for a second think you're irreplaceable!"

"Oh…" the Slug sighed, "for once I felt I had found someone who really knows what it means to be condemned to perpetual motion. But I guess, sliding at the speed I do, I was wrong to assume I'd be eligible to enter your Chain."

"Enter? No! Move in, move out, move on! Don't hesitate, vacate! In a minute! In seconds! Roll up, roll up…"

And so the Chain rattled on.

For some hours later the Slug could still hear the Chain's ringing mantra. Yet it grew fainter and fainter until the Slug, sliding on to new horizons, was finally beyond earshot.

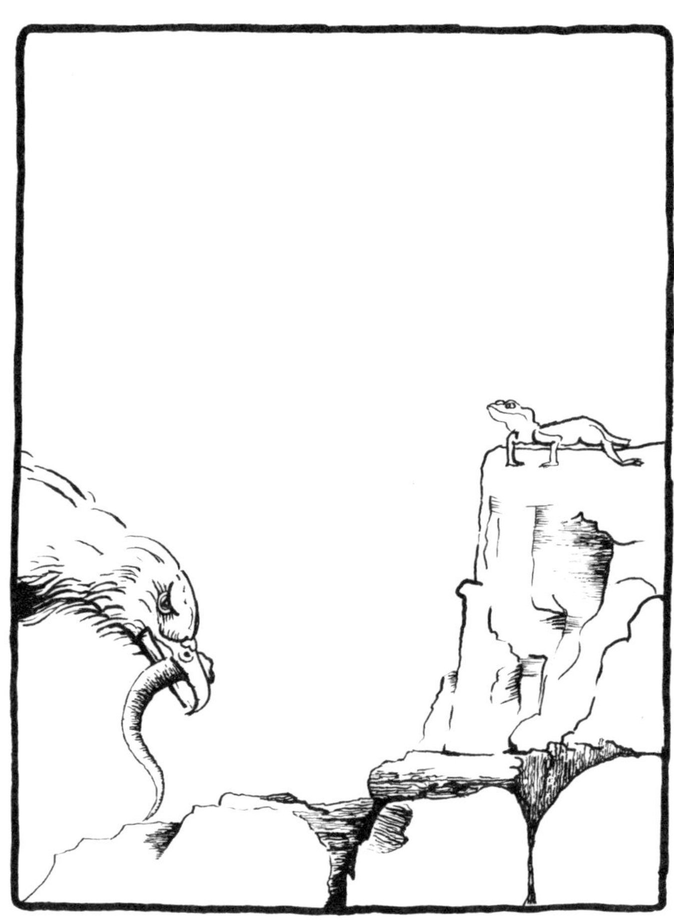

The Lizard & The Eagle

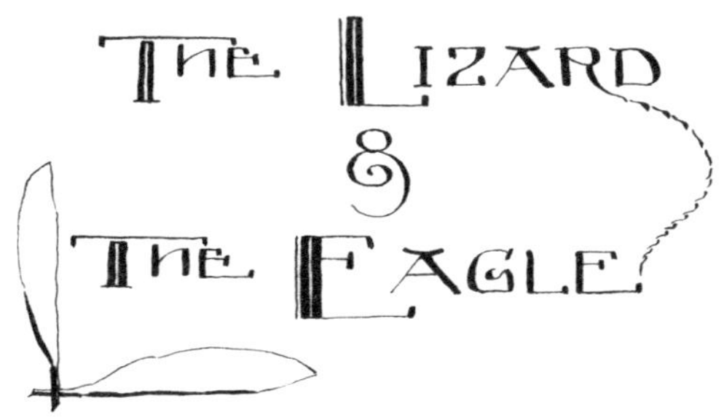

ONE FINE DAY the Lizard was dosing in the sun when the Eagle swooped down from the sky to snatch it. But the Eagle only caught the tail of the Lizard, which the small creature had promptly shed when it saw the Eagle approaching.

"This is ridiculous!" cried the Eagle. "How can it be that I catch my prey and still do not have it for dinner!"

"I am sorry to disappoint you," the Lizard replied from a hole in the rocks where it was hiding. "But I have already given you all that I have to give. There is nothing more I can do for you. If you are unhappy with what you have, I'd say that is entirely your own fault."

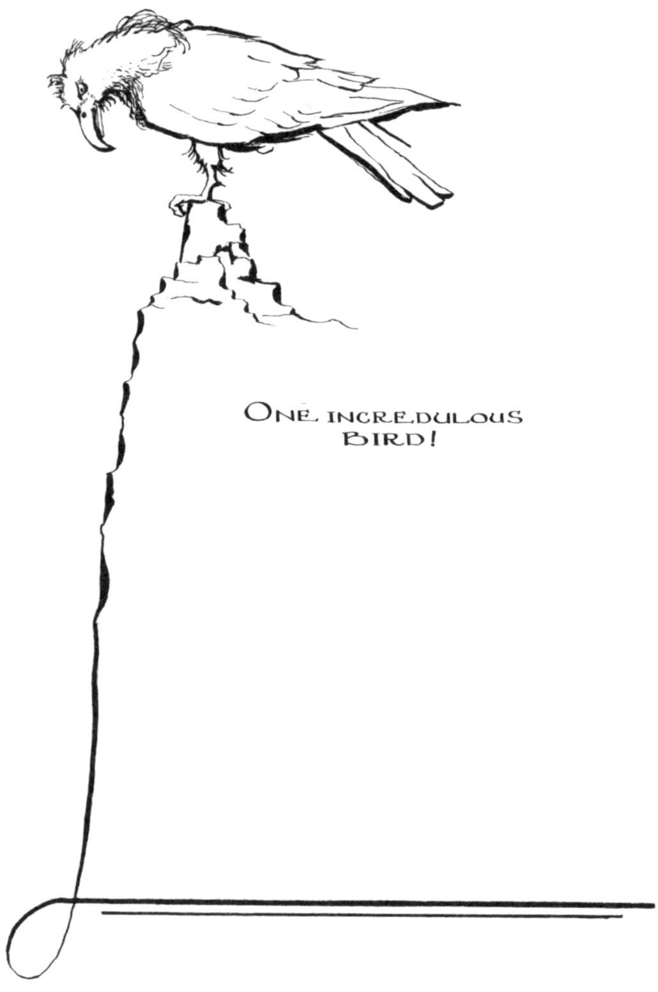
ONE INCREDULOUS
BIRD!

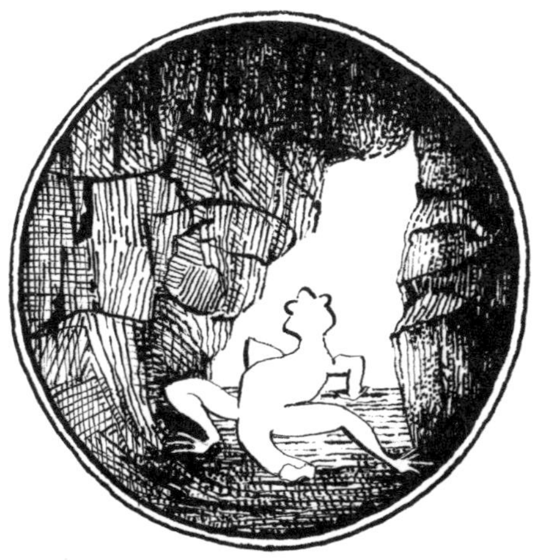

ONE AUDACIOUS
REPTILE!

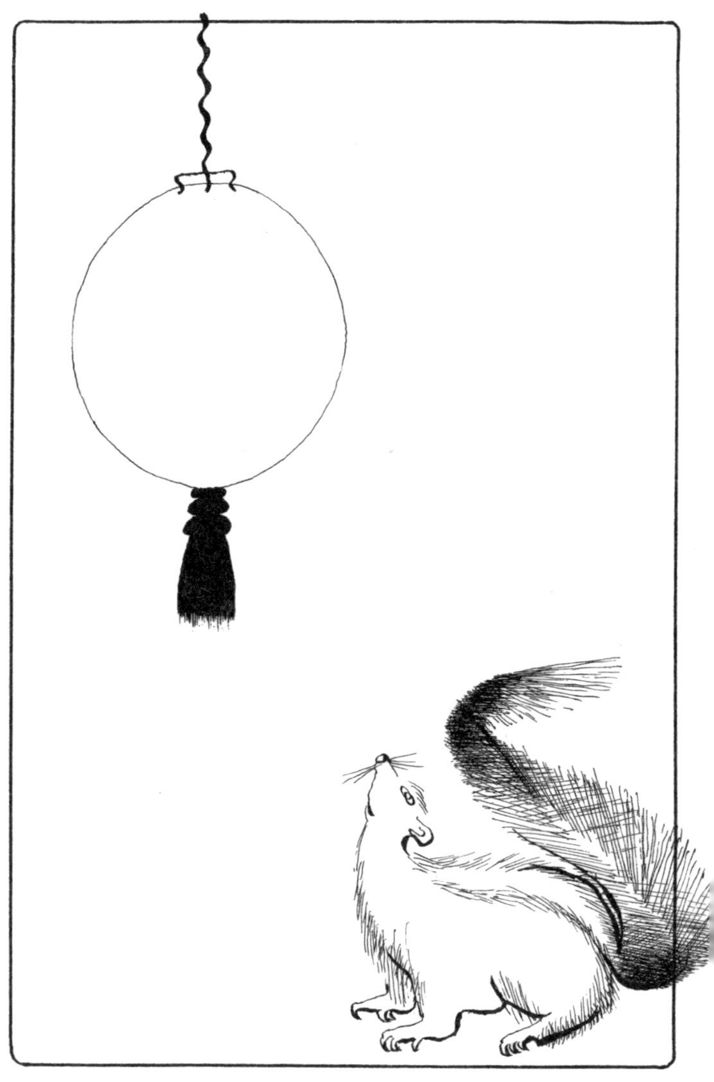

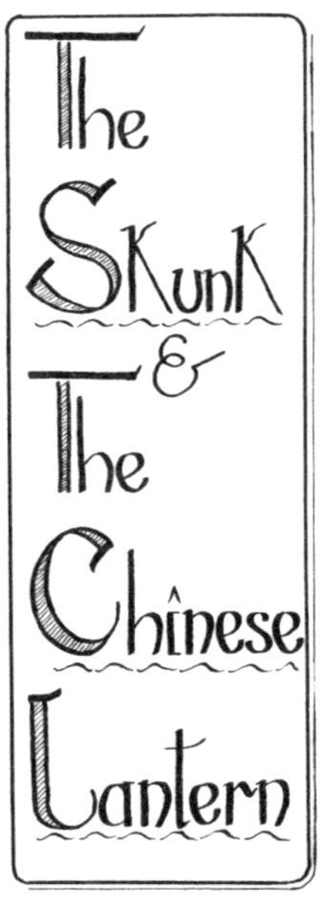

"MY GOODNESS, what a pleasant light you exude," the Skunk enthused gazing up at the Chinese Lantern.

"Thank you. You're welcome..." the Lantern replied, and for an instant the deepening of its glow betrayed the fact that it was blushing. "But if you must know," it continued, "despite all the warmth that I spend, I sometimes do feel oh so hollow on the inside..."

"No!" the Skunk protested, agitatedly pacing to and fro beneath the Lantern. "I find that hard to believe. Of all the lights I have seen, in tone and colour, you strike me as the most perfect. You have great currency if only you could see it. Undervalued, certainly you are, but may I permit myself to suggest that perhaps this view is self-imposed?"

"I appreciate your point," responded the Lantern coyly, "but I really cannot ever be the equal of others."

"Nonsense!" returned the Skunk, "and besides you needn't wallow in sympathy. Shine forth your true value for the world to see!"

Blushing again the Lantern eagerly enquired, "And how is it that you command such high respect?"

"Everyone willingly makes room for me, this is true," said the Skunk, "but I do question the reason. Is it respect? I think not. It's hard to know when, upon my appearance, everyone begs their leave without so much as a good day. I, for one would just love some genuine appreciation."

"I would never leave you like that," replied the Chinese Lantern gently wavering in the evening breeze.

And indeed the Lantern made good on its word. Throughout the night it shone warmly over the scene. And the conversation of the new-found friends was heard well into the early hours.

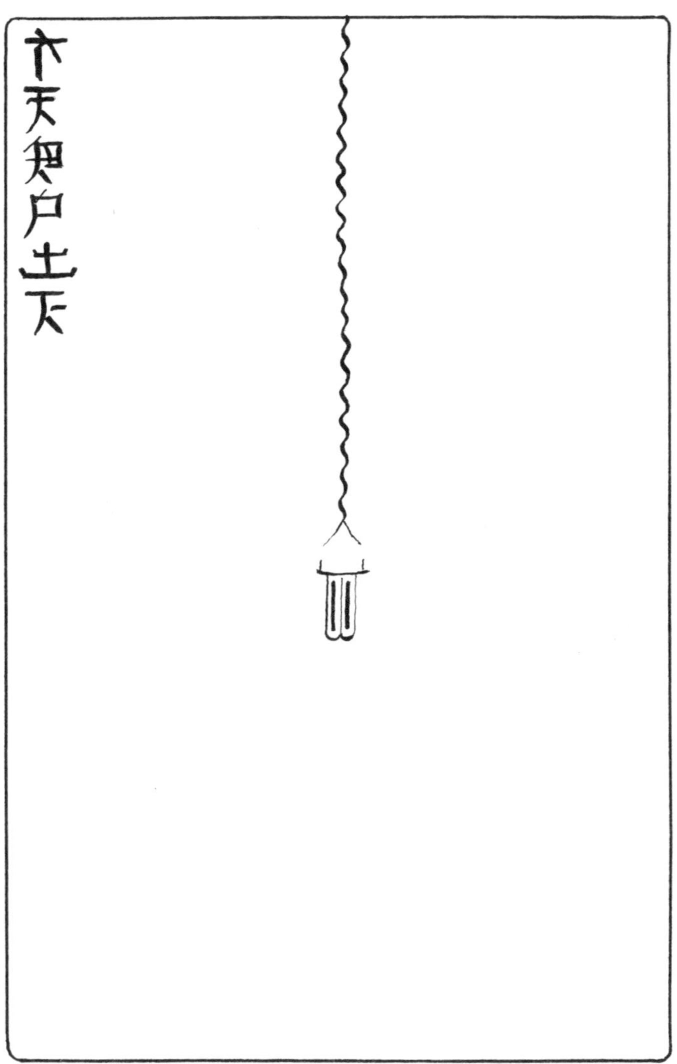

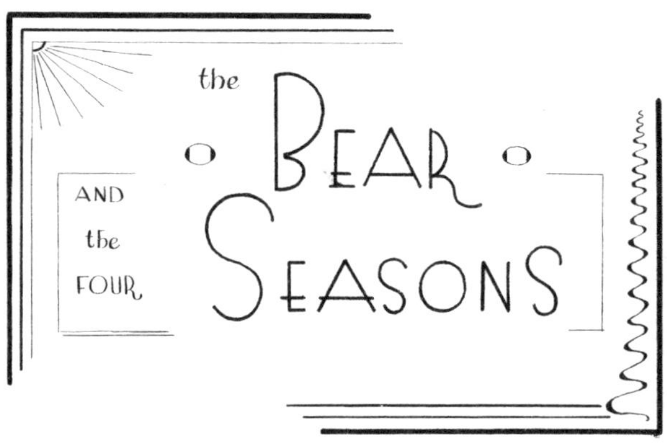

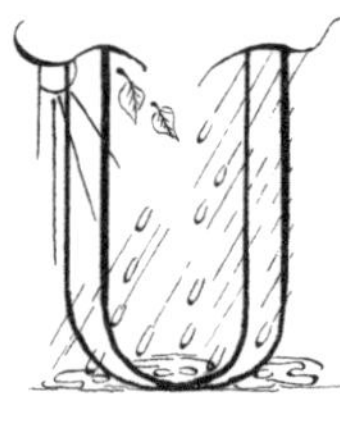PON ONE FINE DAY late in the year the Bear decided to finally meet all the four seasons, and so invited them to his place shortly before his annual sleep. The Spring, Summer and Fall arrived in time and he warmly greeted them.

"Welcome dear Spring!" he exclaimed. "Year after year the tender sunbeams of your mornings have woken me up from my long sleep and have led me out into the world again. I know you well, my friend."

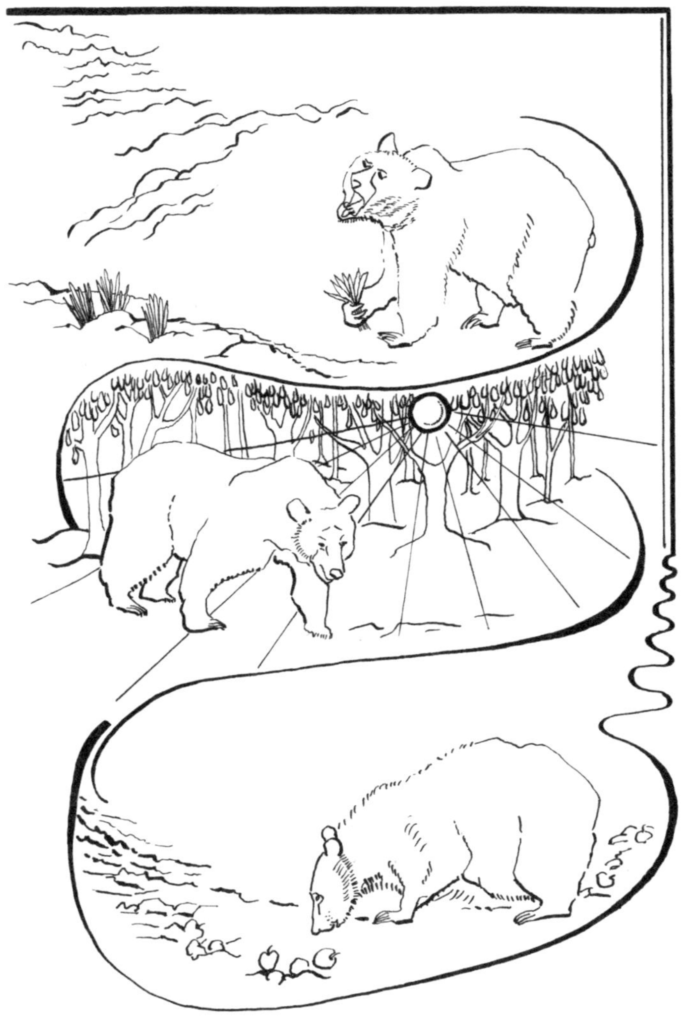

"Welcome dear Summer," he continued. "Year after year I have enjoyed the sunshine and warmth of your days while I was hunting in the forest."

"And welcome dear Fall. During your longer nights I replenish my stocks and prepare myself for the long months of rest."

The evening was spent in merry conversation between friends. Yet, with great disappointment the Bear realised that the one season he had never met but hoped to finally become acquainted with, Winter, had not joined the party. So when the other seasons left for the evening, he made a resolution to end this year unlike previous years, and use all his remaining strength to hold out and wait for Winter to arrive.

Day and night he stayed awake so as not to miss her and while he waited outside his cave he got more and more hungry. In a short time the Bear had devoured all his stocks and, having nothing left to live on, quickly withered away.

On the night he died, Winter walked by his cave, looked at the dead bear and said, "Poor thing! Why could you not see that the friendly seasons gave you life, while the only thing I can give you is death?"

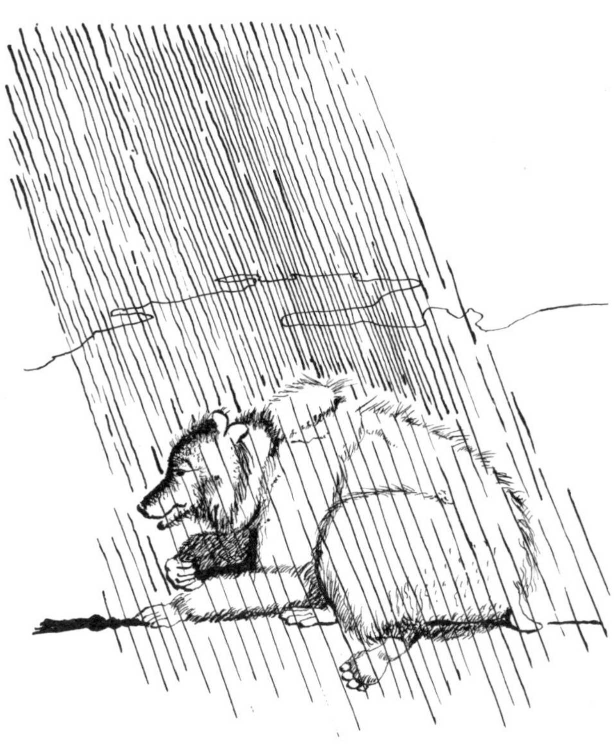

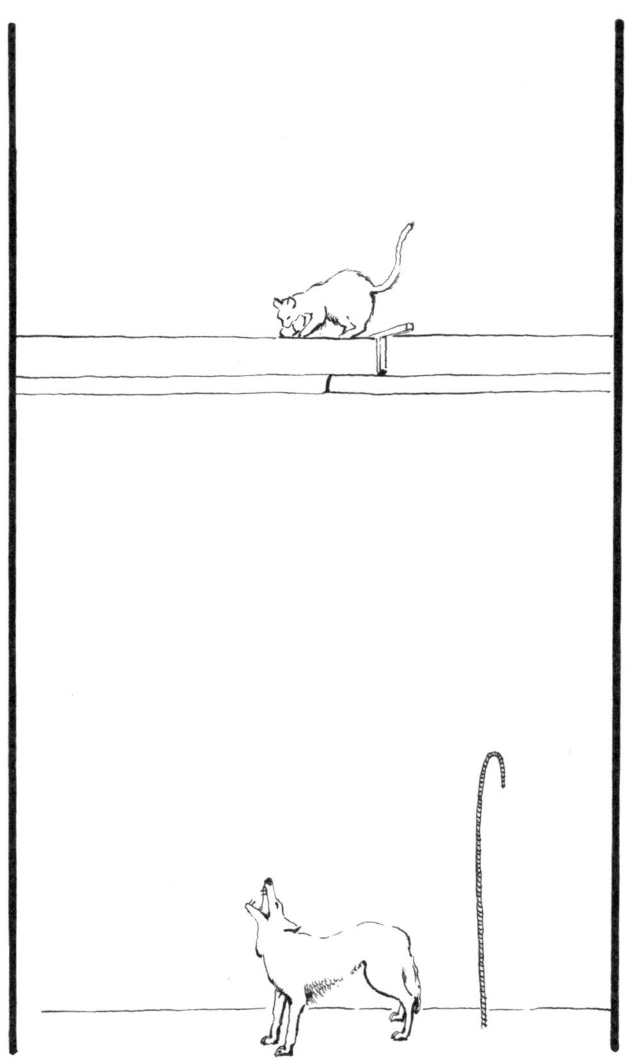

XXII

THE CAT & THE WOLF

THE CAT AND THE WOLF had already crossed paths on the edge of town at night. Insofar as it went, there had been no hostility and meddling was avoided without much effort. One knew to stay in the town and the other in the woods. Matters began to complicate themselves, however, when more and more of the woodlands were cut down to make room for the growth of the city.

Time and again the Wolf, now starving, strayed into the new town settlements where there were still scraps to be scavenged. It wasn't long before the Wolf spied the Cat, thinned to the bone, and perched high on the frame of a half-built house.

Sensing the gravity of the situation, the Cat reluctantly counted its options. It could stay put, safe on the one hand, but on the other... trapped. How long, it thought, could a starving wolf lie in wait? Of all possible options, the most tempting was to simply bolt. But after due consideration the Cat thought better of it.

Conversely, the Wolf was sure it could out-run an undernourished cat, but, since wolves don't climb, the Cat, so long as it did not move, condemned both to waiting. A stalemate! Might they both perish of starvation?

Unable to read the mind of the other beast, the two settled instead on a silent pact, to *keep the status quo*. Both accepted their losses and split.

Thereafter, when they happened to meet, they did so like ships in the night, instinctively letting the other pass to continue their nocturnal pursuits.

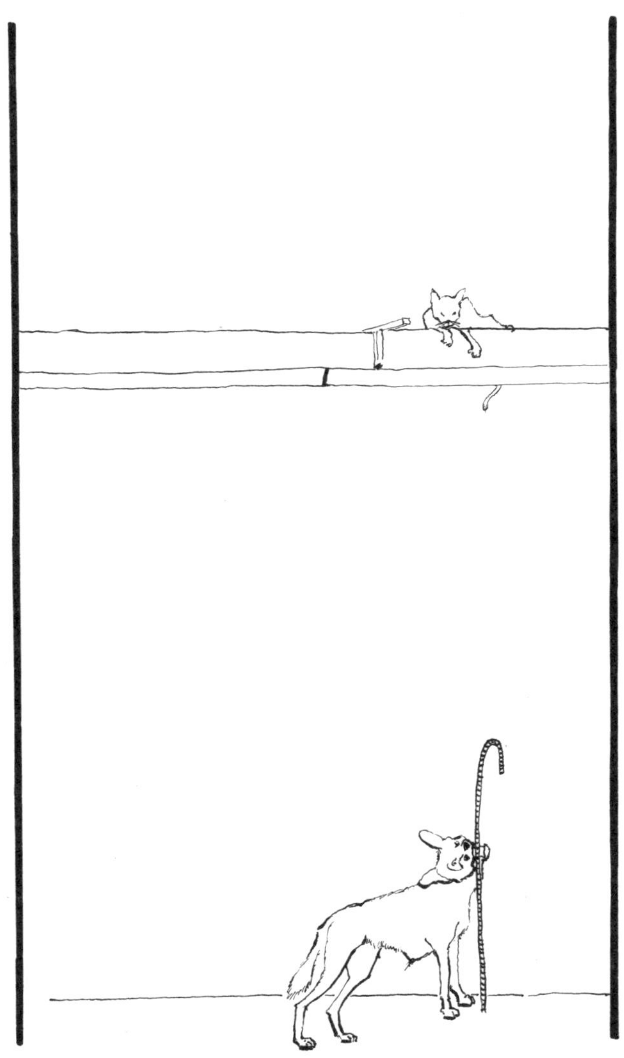

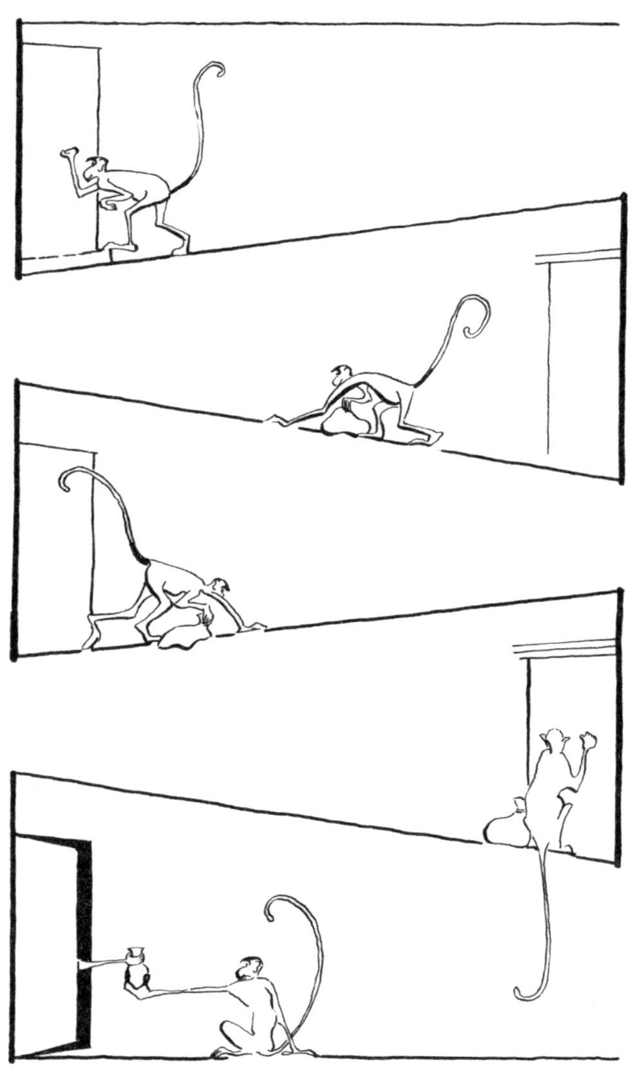

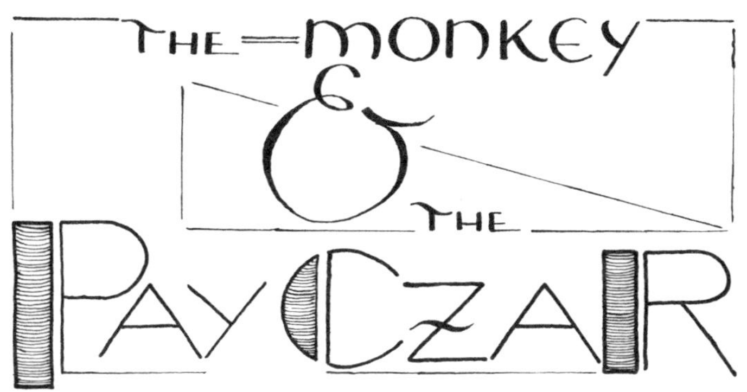

XXIII

THE MONKEY & THE PAY CZAR

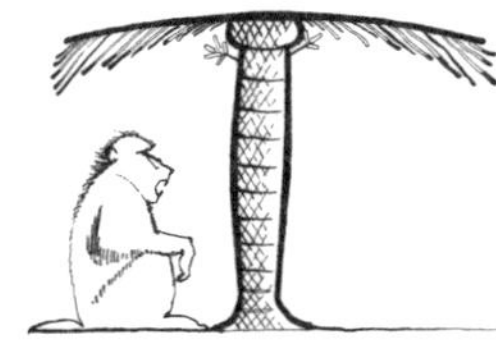

THE MONKEY, mischievous as he is, devised a new scheme. He went to his next-door neighbour, saying, "Give me your savings, and I will return them to you in double in just fifteen days!"

The neighbour, down on his luck, jumped at the proposition and duly handed the Monkey the last of what he had. One week passed and the Monkey again went door knocking, this time a little further down the street. He asked the same question and this time was given a much bigger bag and so, as promised, in fifteen days the first neighbour was re-paid in double, and what was left over was a handsome sum.

And still there was another whole week to door knock! The Monkey lay back and chuckled to himself wondering why no one else had ever thought of such a brilliant scheme before.

Each week he went a little further, door-to-door. All ears were inclined by his silver-spoken offer and few had reason to decline. And so, with the sum he owned and owed having risen higher and higher, eventually, he came a-knocking at the door of the Pay Czar.

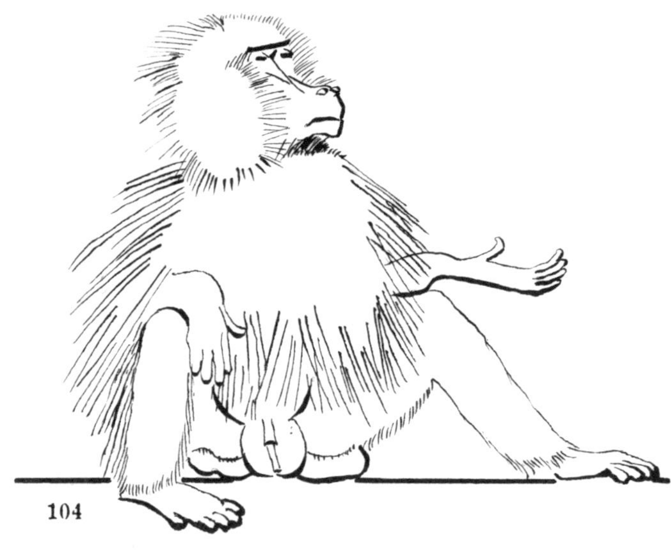

Yet before he could ask him for credit, the Czar softly spoke, "People say you work miracles for them. Ape, let me work one for you. Give me your money and I will triple the sum overnight."

So it was done. And it was the last anyone heard of the Monkey. Smart enough was he to cheat everyone, but wise enough was he to know when to stop.

It's not the law that puts an end to fraud, neither is it bankruptcy. There comes a point when a swindler knows their game is up.

It's the moment they meet their master.

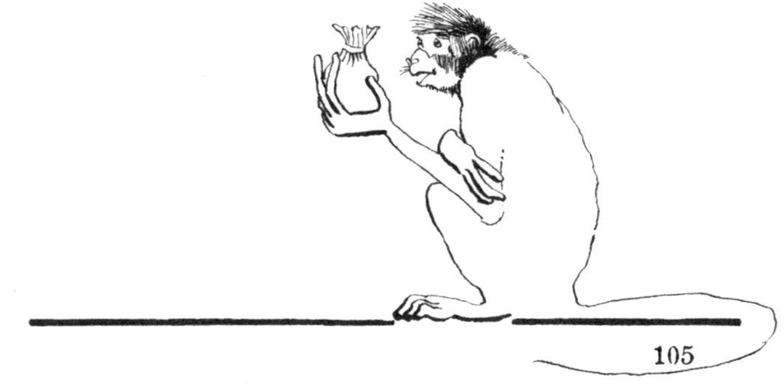

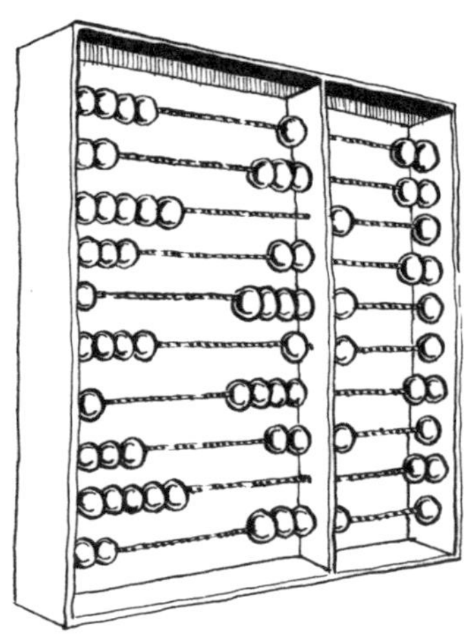

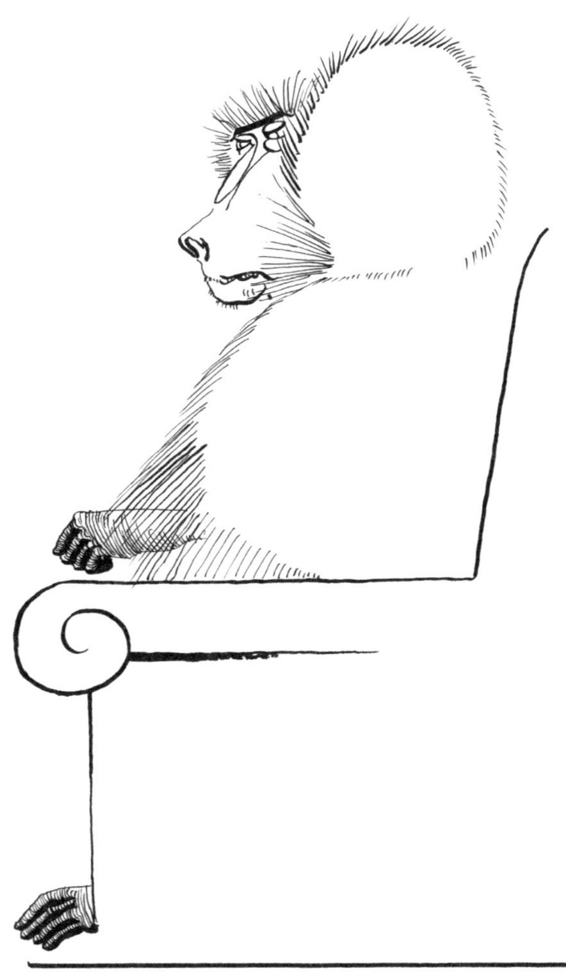

THE MOUSE & the DISTRESSED SELLER

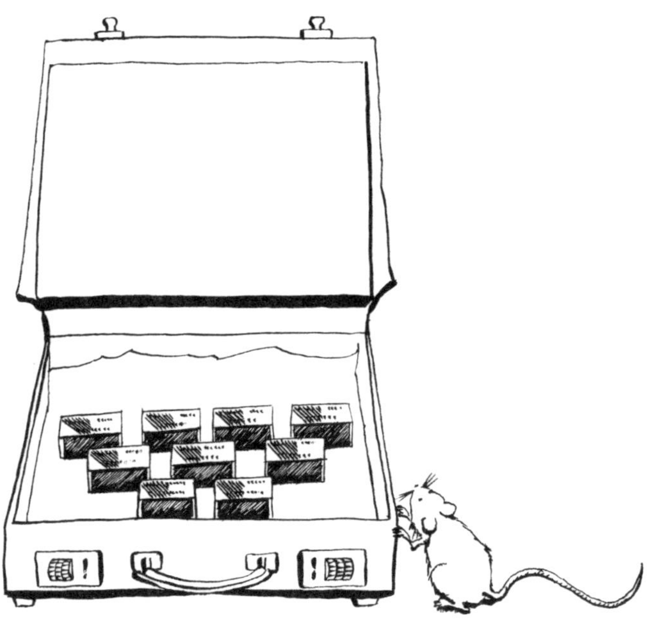

ONE LATE AFTERNOON the Distressed Seller met the Mouse at the door of the Rich Man's mansion.

"My dear little friend, all day I have been trying to sell things but no one wants to buy what I have. My last hope is to talk to this rich man and maybe he can save my day."

"It sounds like you need help," the Mouse said after she had listened to the Distressed Seller's woes. "I will see what I can do for you."

And with these words she disappeared into the mansion. An hour passed before she returned.

"I have good and bad news for you," she cried, sitting on the doorstep. "The good news is that my master likes to acquire things. The bad news is that so many sellers have already been at this doorstep, all with the same things to sell. It seems to me that we already have all we want. If there were, however, one thing of value that we did not already have, my master would want to buy it right away. So what can you give us that we don't have?"

The Distressed Seller paraded his wares, and as this went on the Mouse became more and more despondent.

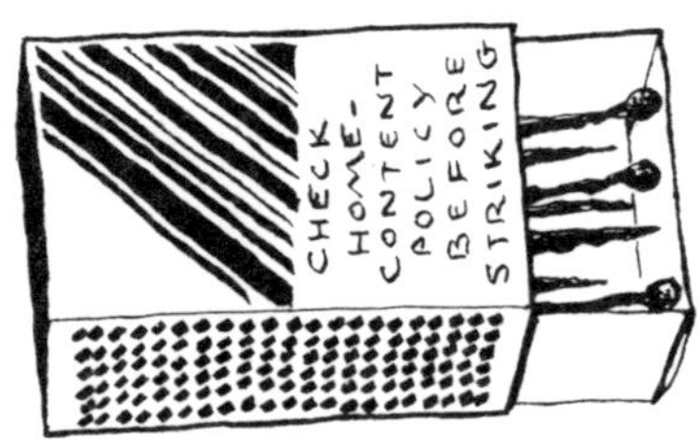

"I have already seen these exact same things."

In a final desperate plea the Seller then begged to speak directly to the Rich Man.

"He is not available as he has gone on an extended business trip," stated the Mouse.

"Then tell me who is here in the building running his affairs?"

"I am," said the Mouse.

Upon hearing this, the Distressed Seller flew into a rage, shouting, "I am not having any more of this!"

He strode past the Mouse into the mansion to see for himself what splendours were amassed.

With eyes wide with shock, he beheld the great halls of the mansion before him practically empty.

"You lied to me!" the Distressed Seller gasped.

"I did not," the Mouse returned calmly. "It is true, the house is all we have here now. But is it not a beautiful place? Unless anyone can offer us something more substantial, pray tell me, why would we forfeit what remains secure?"

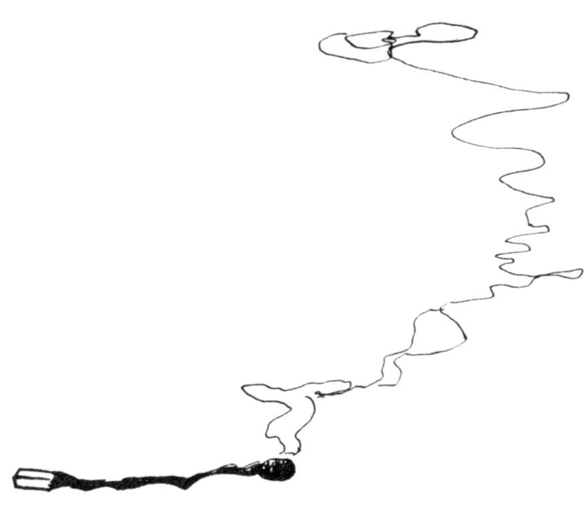

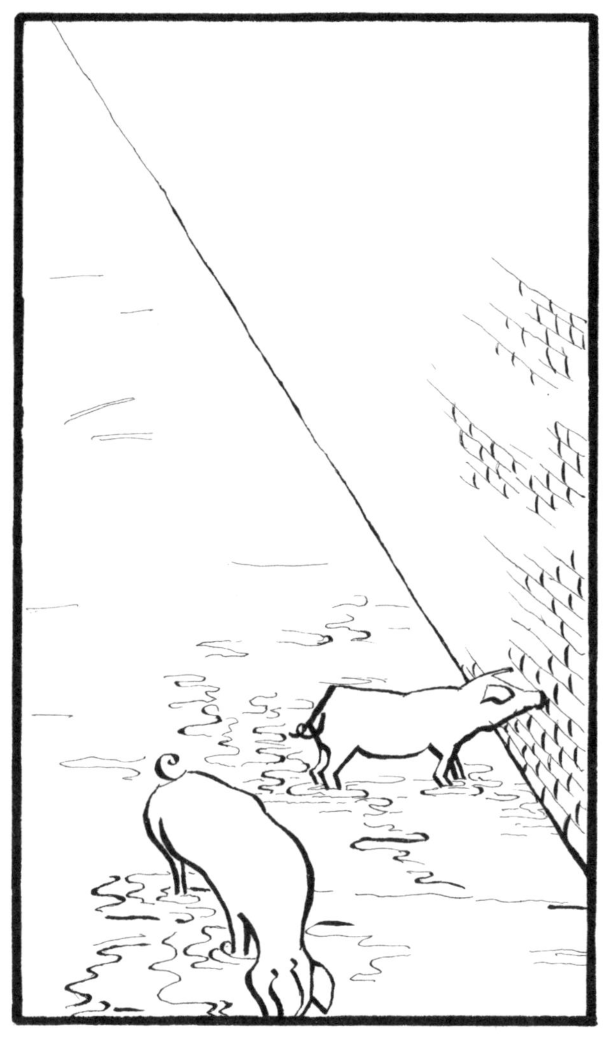

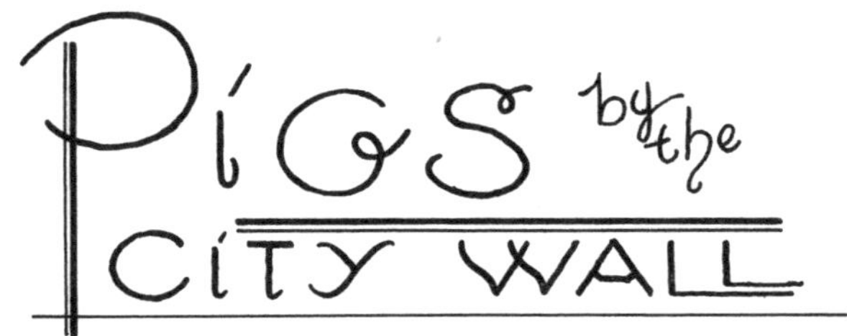

Pigs by the City Wall

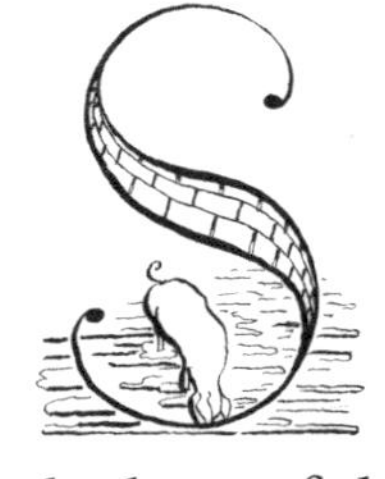

"STABILITY MATTERS," proclaimed the Pigs. "Safety is our first concern. It's why we live at the base of the City Wall. It suits us, this spot, it's secure. That's what we demand."

Yet for all their talk, once in a while a pig just has to do what a pig loves best – root its snout in the muck and indulge in a little digging!

When times are tough, who could blame a simple pig for innocent pastimes?

So they stirred the muck and dug at the base until such time that the City Walls subsided, and collapsed. Yet none suspected the Pigs. In fact they were first in line to lament their loss of protection!

The Pigs then resettled at the revered Palace Gate. After three months, a passing Goat saw them busily digging again.

"In hard times a goat can see the oddest things," it mused in view of the Pigs' newfound status. "No one, it seems, is on their best behaviour. But who wants to rely on civility when times are ripe for folks to push and get straight to what's good for them!"

Thus the Goat was encouraged, and hurried off to strip more bark from the city's trees.

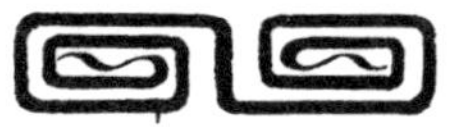

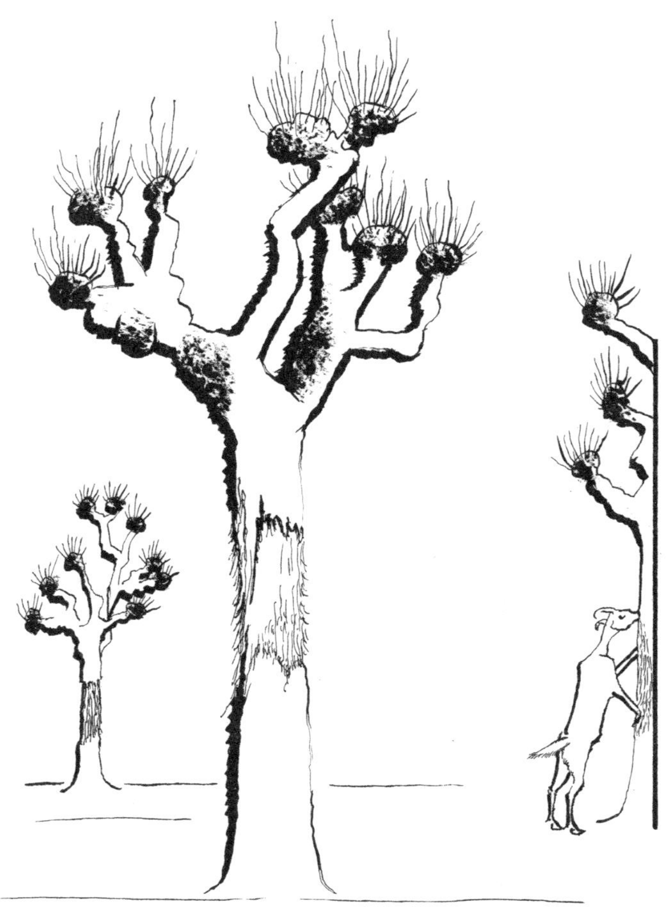

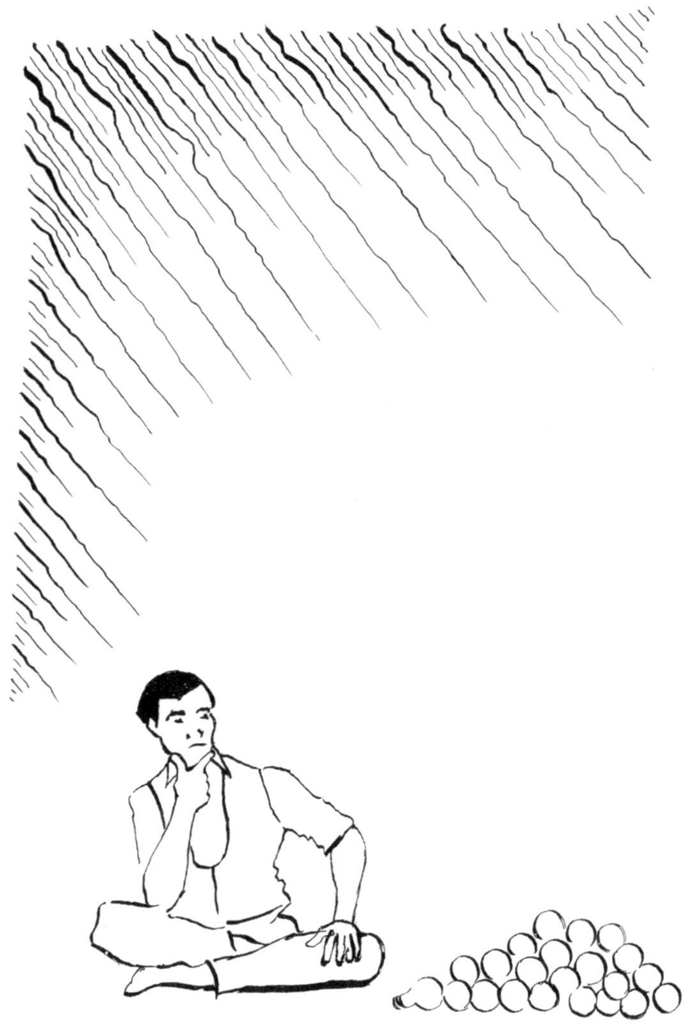

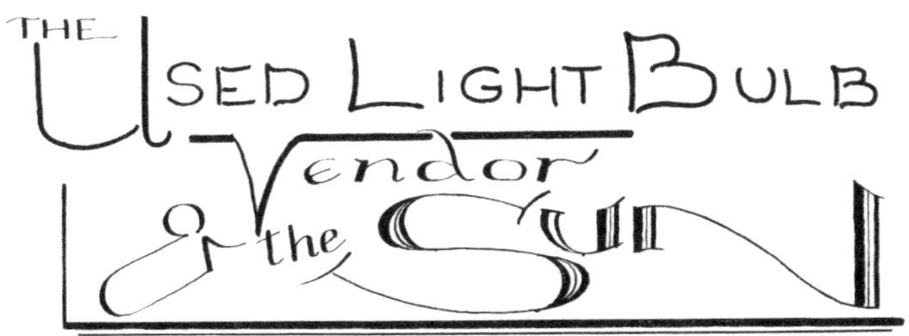 THE USED LIGHT BULB Vendor of the Sun

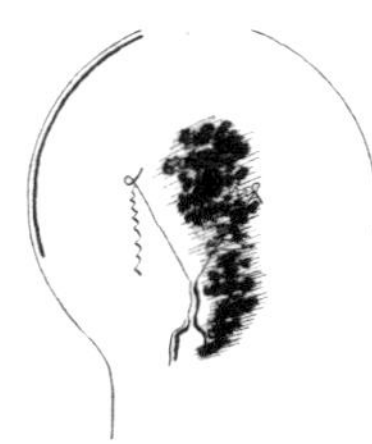

F THE MANY COUNTRIES under the Sun, one was once in scarce supply of everyday goods, for instance, light bulbs. Hence a queer trade prospered in this country, which was seldom practiced elsewhere and never again repeated: the profession of the Used Light Bulb Vendor.

The Vendor sold dead light bulbs to people who would put them in lamps at their workplace, take the good ones home and wait on the bad ones to be changed. It was a great business. Something worth nothing was suddenly worth a little, and at the time, that was a lot. Dead bulbs thus kept being bought, fitted, changed and resold. Bought, fitted, changed and resold...

All the while the Sun was watching, amazed by what it saw. One fine day it came knocking on the Used Light Bulb Vendor's place of business.

"How do you do it?" it burst out when the Vendor opened the door. "I am the Sun. Yet never have I thought of something so brilliant! I give light and know about giving. You, however, have perfected the art of *getting*. Getting something for nothing! Would you share your secret with me?"

"If you wish," spoke the Vendor, shielding his face from the blinding light. "Listen closely. What is empty remains full. What is broken works anew. What is below prime is premium. Hence for the wider good and within their means, the penny turns."

Rattling one of the Vendor's broken bulbs, the Sun remained bewildered. "Riddles fascinate, yet do not explain. Now please reveal your art."

But the practiced Vendor would not, and yet all day long the magnanimous Sun beamed with the prospect of accord.

Hence nought was granted.

And when it could no longer shed fresh luminance, the Sun graciously bade goodnight, leaving the dealer and his bulbs, in the dark.

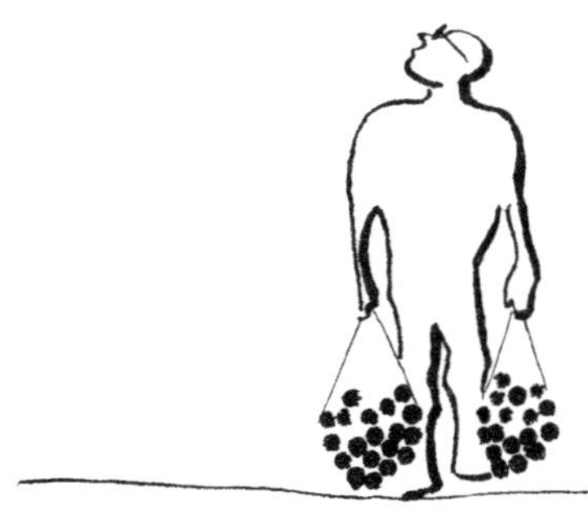

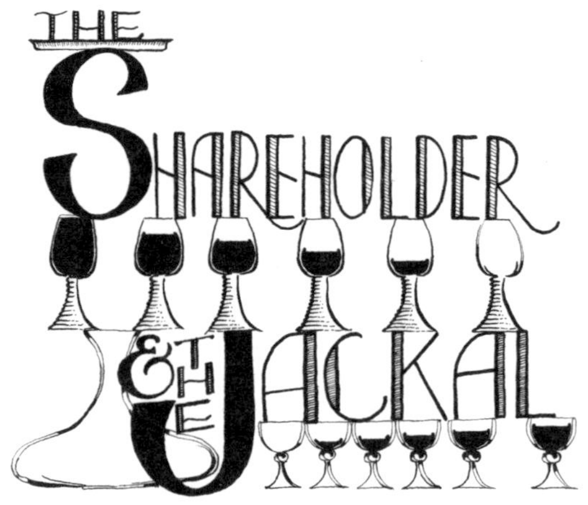

THE SHAREHOLDER & THE JACKAL

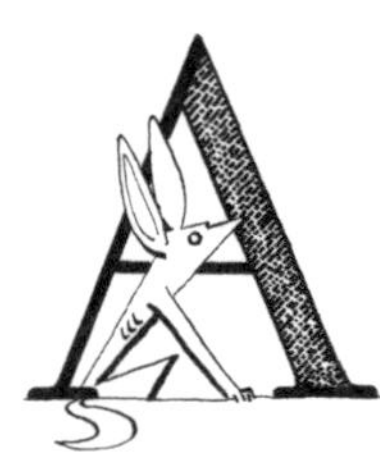

AT THE ANNUAL BANQUET held in honour of the Bull, the Shareholder came to sit next to the Jackal at the dinner table. While the first course was being served, the Jackal inquired with a smile, "I hope you don't mind me asking, but I have never understood how you make your living as a shareholder!"

"No, not at all, please ask. I'd love to explain," the Shareholder replied, happily spooning his soup. "You see the whole idea is that you own a piece

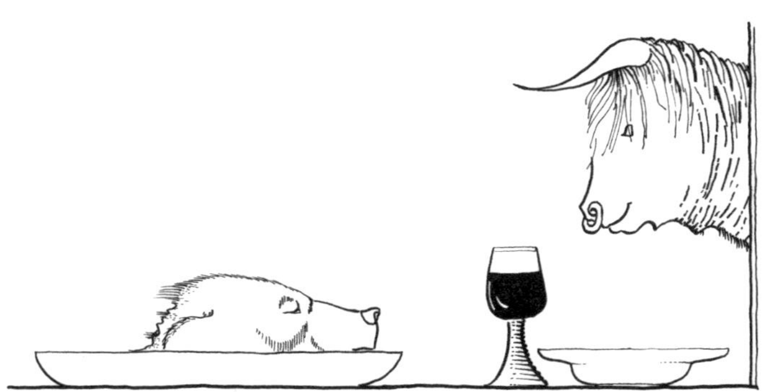

of what other people own, and as long as you don't touch or spend it and let the others do their work, the value of your share gets bigger and bigger."

Upon hearing this, the Jackal frowned, put down his spoon and exclaimed, "Never before have I met such a wise man! But doesn't it make you mad to never touch what you want and could easily have?"

"I am not much interested in withdrawing my share *merely* to take it home to admire," said the Shareholder in a condescending tone.

"Reports from this very evening prove beyond a doubt that the value will keep growing. This is all I need to know."

The next day, confident in his knowledge the Shareholder readily loaned as much money as he could, and with this he bought an even bigger portion of the share.

The honoured Bull seemed more retiring when the annual banquet was held the following year. There did not seem to be enough soup to go around, but there was plenty of wine and merriment. In particularly high spirits that evening was the Shareholder, who soon spotted his friend the Jackal.

"Come sit with me again and I will tell you of the exceedingly good times I have had," he said excitedly.

And so the two sat together at the banqueting table.

After the Shareholder had described his latest ventures the Jackal began to speak.

"I have been thinking a lot since our last conversation," he said, wine glass in hand, "and I have decided I still prefer my trade to yours."

"What exactly is your trade?" enquired the Shareholder.

"You could say it's mixed business," said the Jackal, "but it can involve lending money to people like yourself. When times are uncertain and you have less, what little of real value you still possess you pledge with me to sell. Trust me, you will soon see how good it was that we made friends."

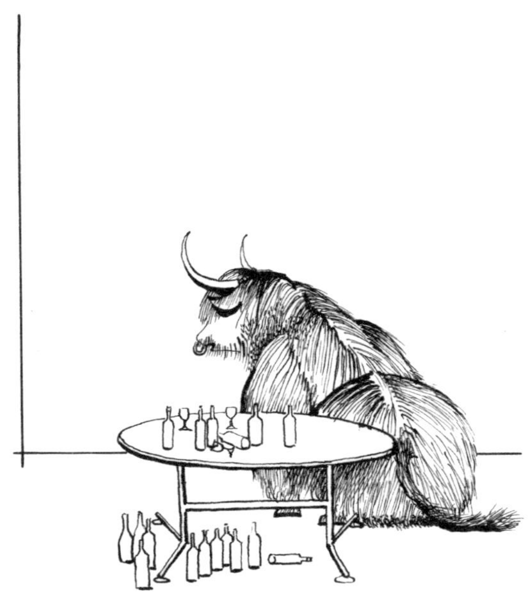

· THE BULL RETIRES ·

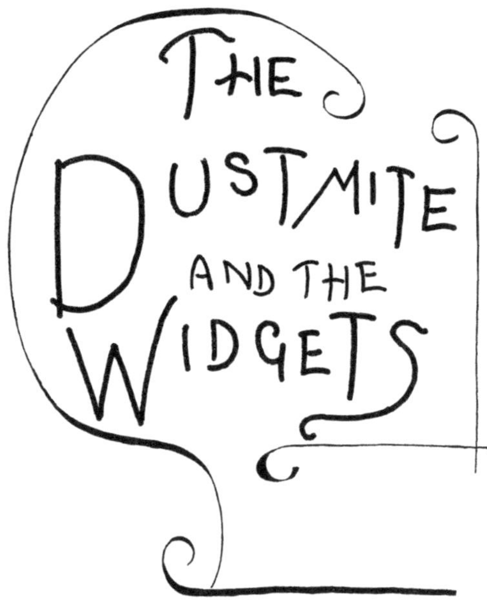

THE DUST MITE had not found time to rest lately. Dust never stopped gathering, and the Mite didn't take its occupation lightly. It kept itself meticulously informed about the dust it digested and the many different fibres, particles and remnants of organic or inorganic matter that could be found in its composition. The Mite thus rightfully prided itself on its insight into the stuff that the world is made of.

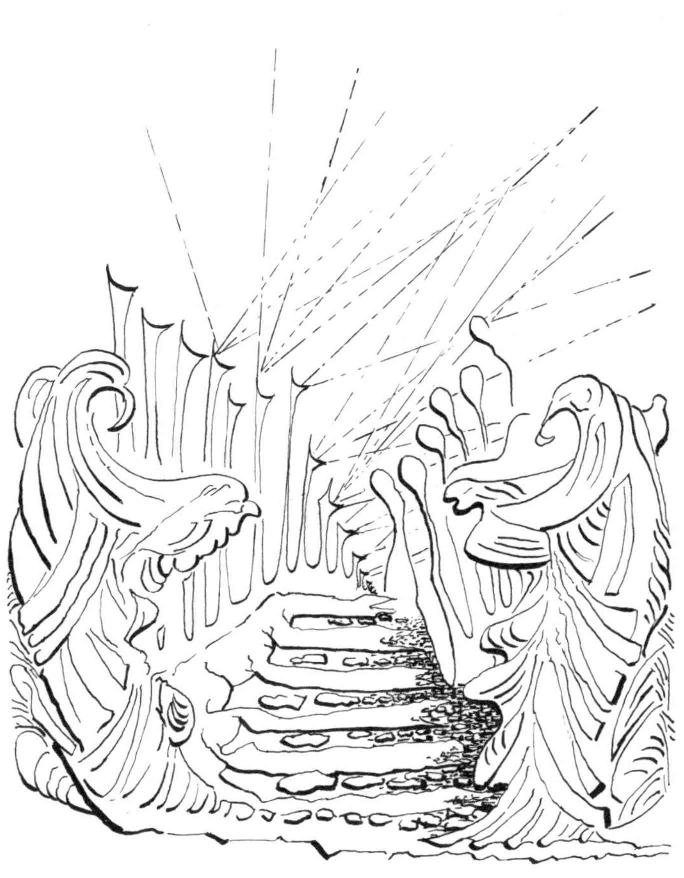

Therefore it was boundlessly surprised when it first met the Widgets. Trying to make out someone to address in their featureless mass the Mite exclaimed:

"Who are you?"

The Widgets appeared in great numbers but spoke with one voice. "We," they boomed, "are whatever you want us to be. We have no preference, no state or creed. We're aligned with none. We have no mother tongue. We have no form you see."

Accustomed to the murmur of dust, the Mite was nearly deafened by the volume of the Widgets' address.

"You, sir, sift dust for a living, but we, we are the cement of the universe. We are sold and bought. Without us, all affairs come to nought!"

And with that they marched off, keeping in neat rank and file, yet changing shape every other instant.

Eager to learn more, the Mite left its dusty home to follow the Widgets.

"But how," it persisted, "can you claim to be what everything is made of, when you show that nothing is solid and all is in flux?"

"You must understand," spoke the Widgets, "that in the commerce of life, change is the one constant that circulates. Any one unit can be any other, and there won't ever be anything missing or lost…"

"Oh… oh… oh…!" were the Mite's last words. By following the Widgets, it had entered a universe where nothing faded, nothing turned to dust and hence nothing was there to nourish a humble Mite.

So it withered away, and the Widgets marched on.

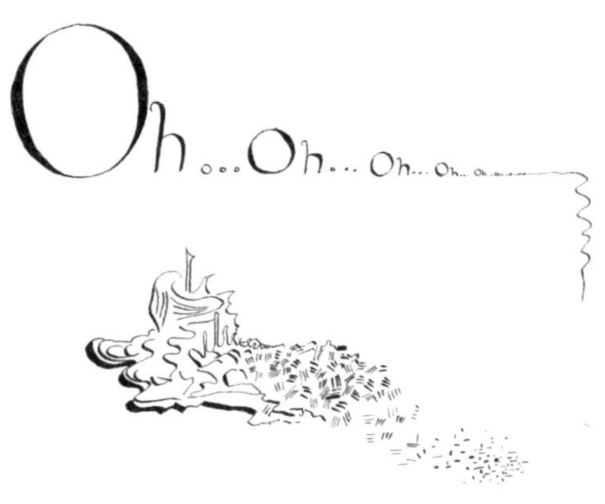

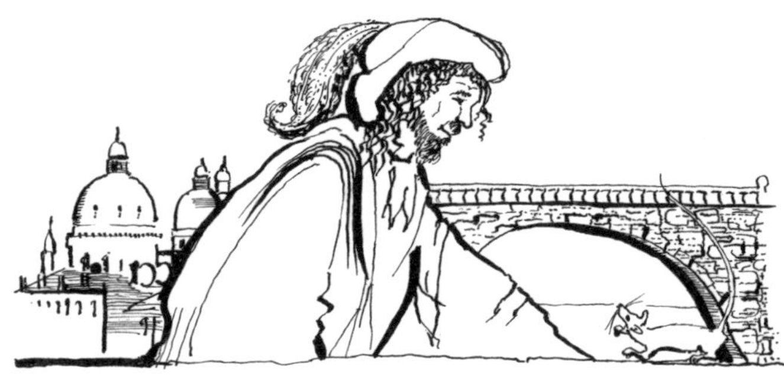

T WAS in the early hours of the morning when the Cavalier was returning to his lodgings that he chanced upon the Rat under a bridge by a lonely canal. When their gazes met, they inspected each other for a moment.

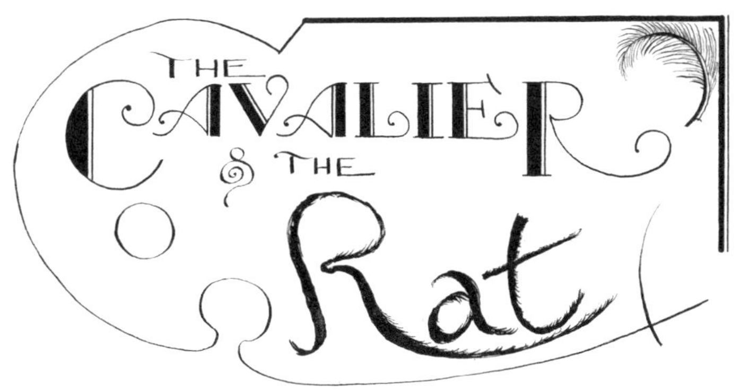

The Rat broke the silence and, with its low raspy voice, remarked, "On our way home, aye, are we?"

"Indeed we are, are we not?" the Cavalier replied, his voice strained from the excesses of liquor and tobacco.

Hearing how hoarse their voices sounded, the Cavalier laughed.

So did the Rat. And with a few rapid moves, made its way up, over some boxes, onto the top of a barrel, to get close to eye level with its new acquaintance.

"And as indeed we are," the Rat resumed, "the time would seem right to take stock. What are the night's gains and losses?"

"Events of a single night are rarely something to go by, don't you think?" croaked the Cavalier. "It's the long returns that count, so you keep your composure and your irons in the fire."

"Yet, the night is long and fortunes can be changed in an instant," quipped the Rat.

"My friend, your words belie admirable passions, but misfortune is the slight of hand revealed, out of haste, too soon. It ruins the most promising advances."

"But how can you have confidence that success is yours, when you don't take every chance to win it?" enquired the Rat in an anxious tone.

"Excuse me for saying this," declared the Cavalier, "but it's here you rodents invariably err. You think fate is shaped by passion. Yet good fortune never arrives, it only returns to those who have always possessed it. Why do the less fortunate fail to grasp that fate can't be forced? You can try of course. But I urge you not. Now get some rest, Rat, goodnight!"

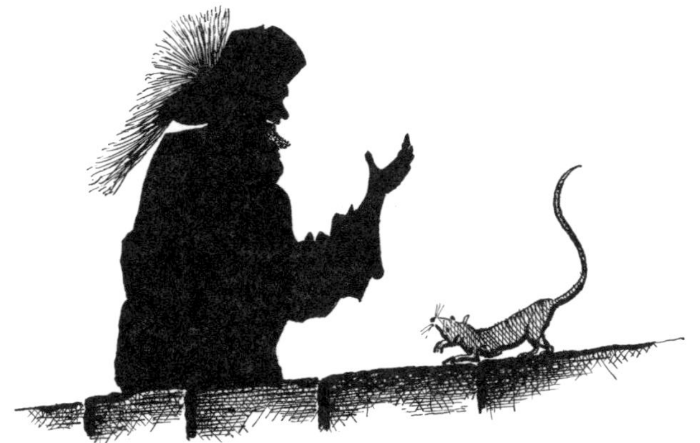

Good Night!

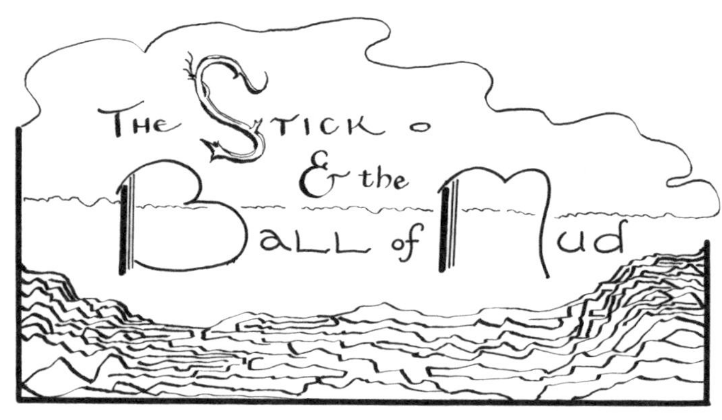

"HEY YOU, Stick ahead, get out of the way!" cried the Ball of Mud as it was fast approaching, rolling down the side of the hill to the bottom, where the Stick was stuck in the ground.

No reply from the Stick.

Only seconds before impact, screaming in fear at the stolid Stick, the Ball begged, "I implore you, Stick, move, or it'll be the end of both of us!"

"How do you know?" the Stick finally spoke, calm and assured. "You never met me before... maybe the two of us do have a future?"

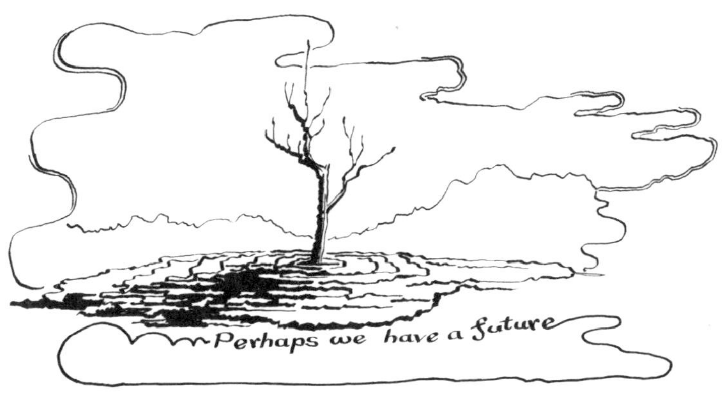

Most gracious this pronouncement was and not bad for a stick's last words, for right after it spoke, it was broken apart by the blow of mud shattering against it.

From the top of the hill, Zeus watched the scene and sighed, "May the open minded one day realise that it is not a bad decision to sometimes step aside and let life pass them by..."

• • •

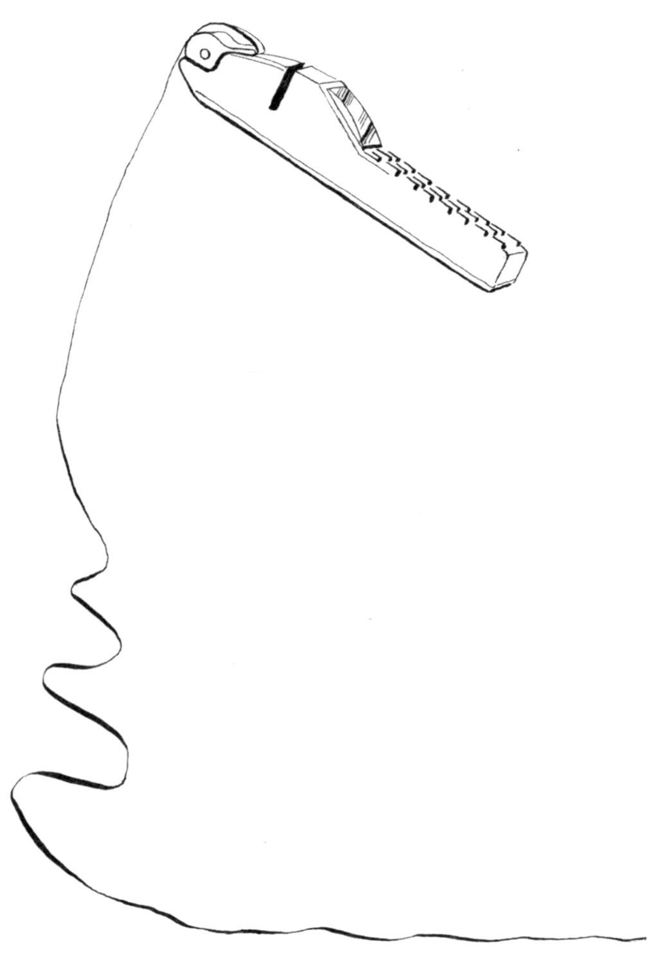

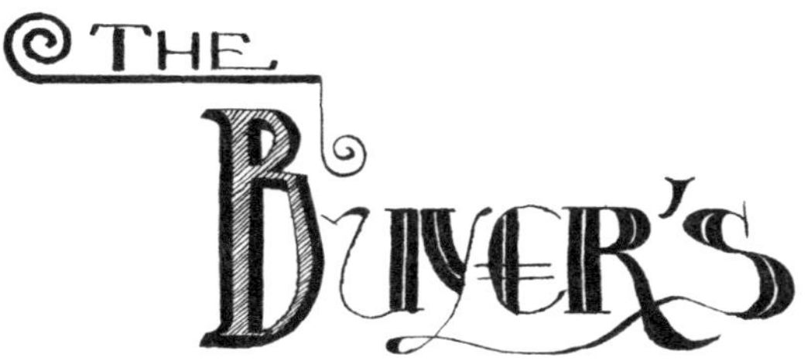

THE BUYER'S REMORSE

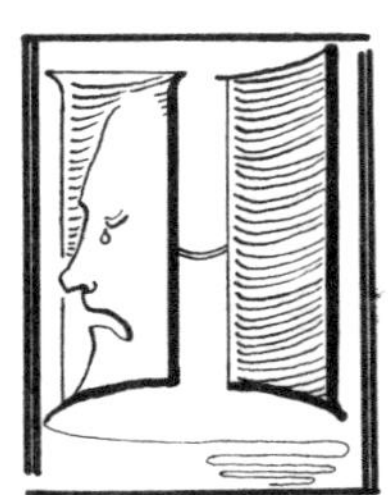

EADING HOME from the auction house one day went the Buyer, touting his latest pride and joy. Heedless to traffic he marched, euphoric in the golden moment. Along the way he garnered the curiosity of others. For many were eager to know of the Buyer's latest conquest. At every street corner they stood, impressed indeed that he possessed the finest money could buy. Though there was not much to see that day, except for the packaging.

Bidding good day to the last well-wisher, he closed his front door to be alone with his admired acquisition. However, all the inquisitive stares and all the well-meaning smiles from the day's parading, could not console the Buyer once he began to open the package. His prize had been wrapped layer upon layer with such care and art that removing it required patience. None of this he had.

Anxious to confirm the sobriety of his recent purchase, he did what he could most easily do and pulled out the receipt from his pocket.

"Now, this document," he thought to himself, "will without further ado, satisfy my wish to be sure that I receive the best I can ever get!"

But who is to measure the horror he felt when all the paper showed was the sum he had paid and the signature he put down to confirm the transaction. Nothing more, not even the slightest proof of him having acquired anything, apart from a box of exquisite wrappings!

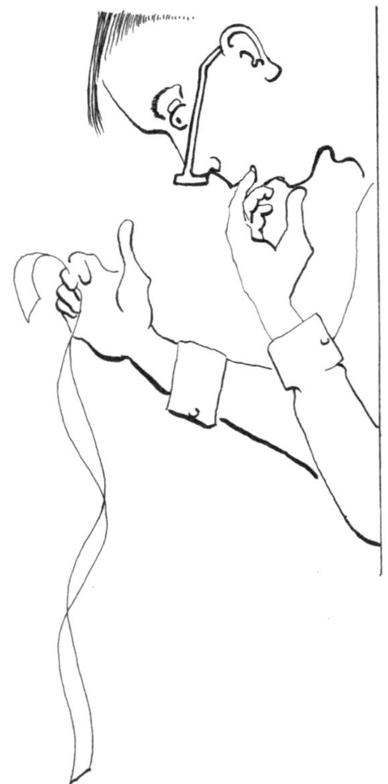

Unwilling to check the box for fear of the biggest disappointment, yet equally unable to put down the paper that hinted at that very prospect, the Buyer remained in the place he was, arrested by fear and anticipation. And among those walking the streets of the city he was nevermore seen.

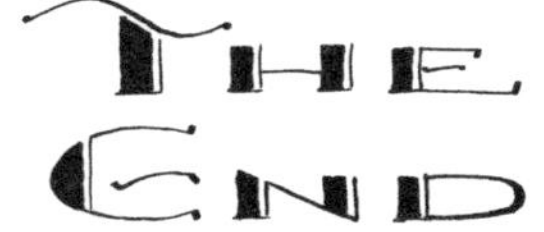

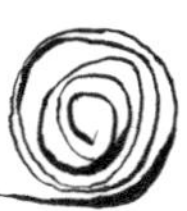

Thanks to

Saâdane Afif
Lionel Bovier
Melinda Braathen
Steven Brower
Dick Frizzell
Marcus Lütkemeyer
Marie Marchal
Anamarie Michnevich
Bas Mühren
Warren Olds
Gwynneth Porter
Laura Preston
Bio Schmidt-Bleek
Cornelia Schmidt-Bleek
Alan Stevenson
Serjoscha Stevenson
Alexander Strengers
Raphaela Vogel

The ARTIST, The MOTHER, The CRITIC, & the SPIRIT MAKER

Colophon

Animal Spirits
Fables

Written, collected and re-told
in the parlance of our time

by Michael Stevenson
and Jan Verwoert

Illustrated by Michael and Margaret Stevenson
Graphic design and production: Christoph Keller
Print: DZA Druckerei zu Altenburg GmbH

This book is part of the
Christoph Keller Editions series.

2013

Published by

JRP | Ringier
Limmatstrasse 270, CH-8005 Zurich
T +41 (0) 43 311 27 50, F +41 (0) 43 311 27 51
E info@jrp-ringier.com, www.jrp-ringier.com

ISBN: 978-3-03764-137-8 (JRP | Ringier)

JRP | Ringier books are available internationally at selected bookstores
and from the following distribution partners:

Switzerland: AVA Verlagsauslieferung AG, www.ava.ch
France: Les Presses du réel, www.lespressesdureel.com
Germany and Austria: Vice Versa Distribution GmbH,
www.vice-versa-distribution.de
UK and other European countries:
Cornerhouse Publications, www.cornerhouse.org/books
USA , Canada, Asia, and Australia:
ARTBOOK | D.A.P., www.artbook.com

Clouds
PO Box 68-187, Auckland 1145. Aotearoa New Zealand
T +64 (9)309 2604
E hello@clouds.co.nz, www.clouds.co.nz

ISBN 978-0-9582981-6-2 (Clouds)

Animal Spirits is distributed by Clouds and
Contemporary Art Books Australasia (www.caba.org.au)
in New Zealand and Australia.

This book has been supported by
Creative New Zealand Toi Aotearoa.

CHRISTOPH KELLER EDITIONS

Published in a limited print run, this series of artists' books and conceptual art publications, edited and selected by Christoph Keller, aims to explore the bandwidth of artistic book-making and the mediation of contemporary art in the printed format of the book.

Other titles in this series:

Emmanuelle Antille, *Tornadoes of My Heart* · Helen Mirra, *Cloud, the, 3* · Jonathan Meese & Slavoj Zizek, *Ernteschach dem Dämon* · Peter Piller, *Teilzeitkraft* · Mungo Thomson, *Negative Space* · Stuart Bailey & Ryan Gander, *Appendix Appendix* · Peter Piller, *Nijverdal/Hellendoorn* · Matias Faldbakken, *Not Made Visible* · Johannes Wohnseifer, *Werkverzeichnis, 1992–2007* · Archiv Peter Piller, *nimmt Schaden* · Mai-Thu Perret, *Land of Crystal* · Julien Berthier, *Nothing Special* · Archiv Peter Piller, *Zeitung* · Michael Stevenson, *Celebration at Persepolis* · Jonathan Monk, *Complete Ilford Works* · Zilla Leutenegger, *Zilla and the 7th Room* · Aglaia Konrad, *Desert Cities* · Jeanne Faust, *Outlandos* · Loris Gréaud, *Cellar Door* · Claudia & Julia Müller, *Habitus vs. Habitat: Primaten* · Boris Groys & Andro Wekua, *Wait to Wait* · Korpys/Löffler, *Die Sehnsucht nach Glück ...* · Anna Lea Hucht, *Sprich mit Deiner Seele* · Jonathan Monk, *Studio Visit* · Yann Sérandour, *Inside the White Cube, Overprinted Edition* · Falke Pisano, *Figures of Speech* · Heidi Specker & Theo Deutinger, *Help Me, I'm Blind* · Philip Lachenmann, *Some Scenic Views* · Ryan Gander, *Catalogue Raisonnable Vol. 1* · Hinrich Sachs, *Lost Once More* · Stefan Marx, *I guess I shouldn't be telling you* · Rita McBride, *Westways* · Mischa Kuball/Harald Welzer, *New Pott – Neue Heimat im Revier* · Gitte Villesen, *The story is not all mine, nor told by me alone* · Jakob Kolding, *Shifting Realities* · Slavs and Tatars, *Molla Nasreddin* · Archiv Peter Piller, *Kraft* · Kerstin Brätsch/ Adele Röder, *Das Institut. Triennial Report 2011–2009* · Iñaki Bonilas, *J.R. Plaza Archive* · Oriol Vilanova, *They Cannot Die* · Come on in my Kitchen – The Robert Johnson Book

Published by

JRP|Ringier

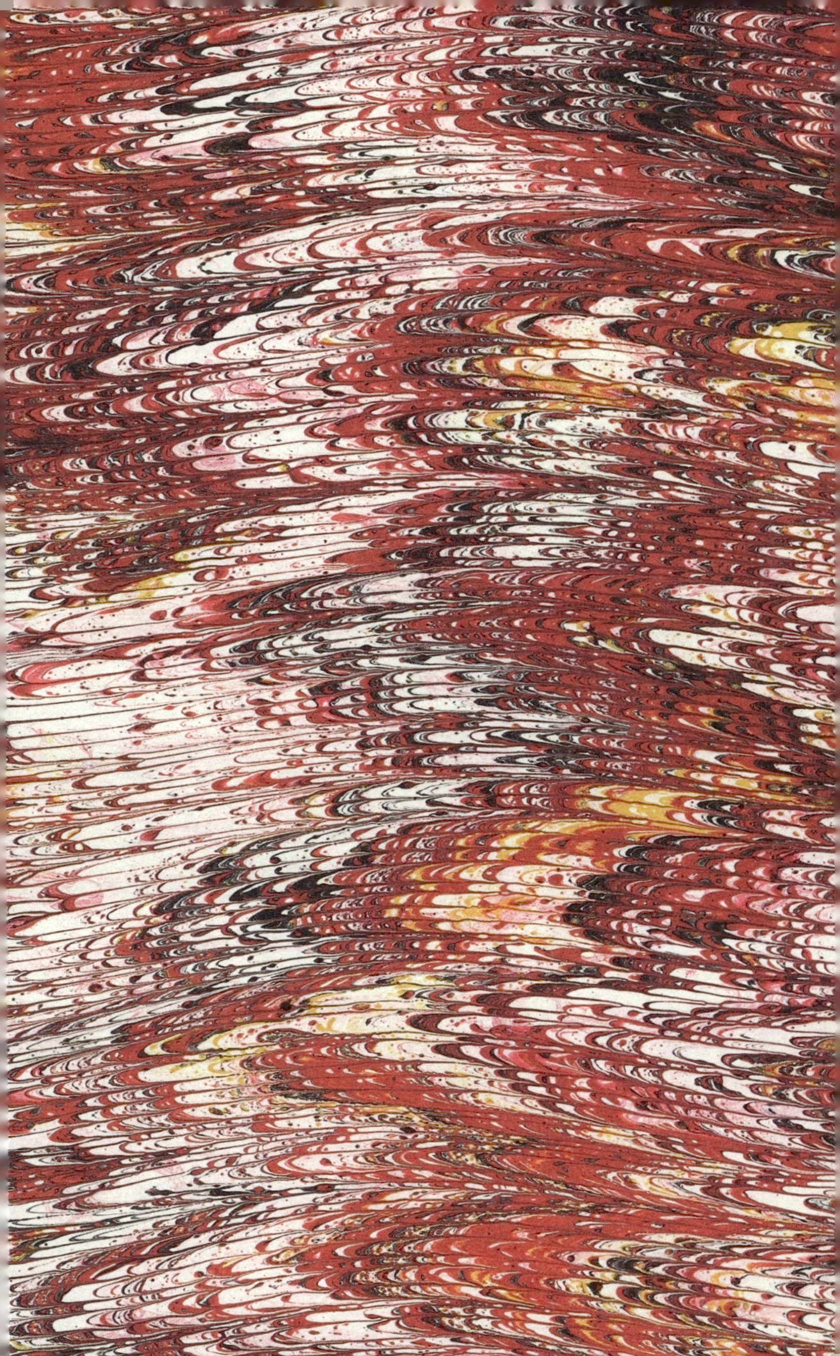

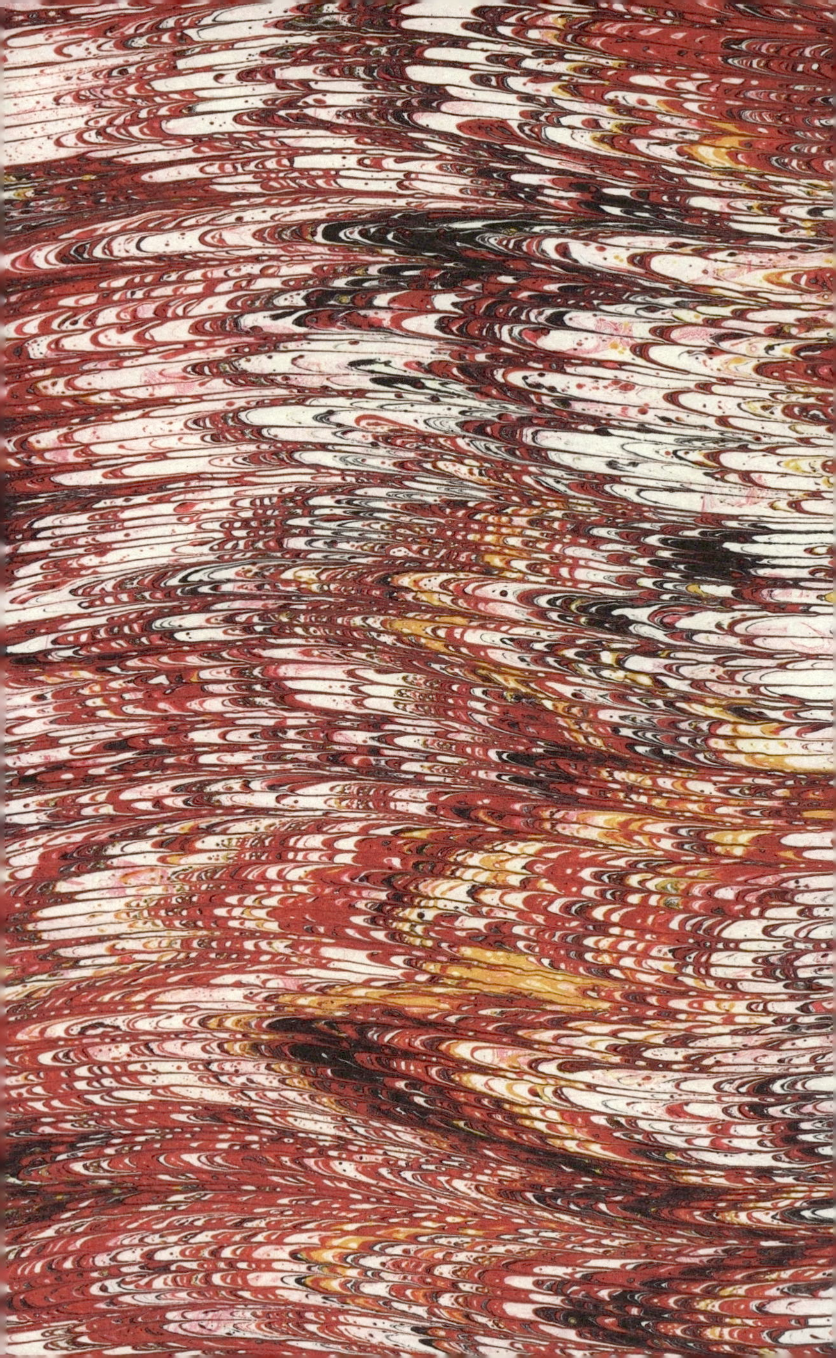